BEST OF

Milan

Alison Bing

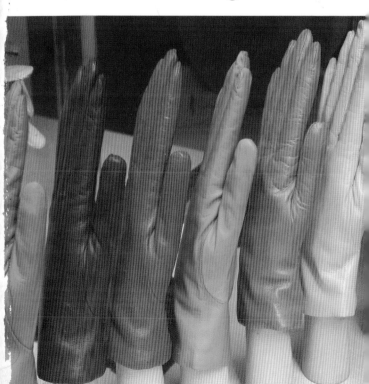

Colour-Coding & Maps

Each chapter has a colour code along the banner at the top of the page which is also used for text and symbols on maps (eg all venues reviewed in the Highlights chapter are orange on the maps). The fold-out maps inside the front and back covers are numbered from 1 to 4. All sights and venues in the text have map references; eg, (2, C3) means Map 2, grid reference C3. See p96 for map symbols.

Prices

Multiple prices listed with reviews (eg [$10/5]) usually indicate adult/concession admission to a venue. Concession prices can include senior, student, member or coupon discounts. Meal cost and room rate categories are listed at the start of the Eating and Sleeping chapters, respectively.

Text Symbols

- ☎ telephone
- ✉ address
- 🖳 email/website address
- € admission
- ☺ opening hours
- ⓘ information
- Ⓜ metro
- 🚌 bus
- Ⓟ parking available
- ♿ wheelchair access
- ✗ on site/nearby eatery
- 🚼 child-friendly venue
- Ⓥ good vegetarian selection
- ⚓ ferry
- 🚋 tram
- 🚗 car
- ✸ air conditioning
- ⊗ non smoking rooms

Best of Milan
2nd edition – January 2007
First published – January 2005

Published by Lonely Planet Publications Pty Ltd
ABN 36 005 607 983

Australia Head Office, Locked Bag 1, Footscray, Vic 3011
☎ 03 8379 8000, fax 03 8379 8111
🖳 talk2us@lonelyplanet.com.au
USA 150 Linden St, Oakland, CA 94607
☎ 510 893 8555, toll free 800 275 8555
fax 510 893 8572
🖳 info@lonelyplanet.com
UK 72–82 Rosebery Ave, Clerkenwell, London
EC1R 4RW
☎ 020 7841 9000, fax 020 7841 9001
🖳 go@lonelyplanet.co.uk

This title was commissioned in Lonely Planet's London office and produced by: **Commissioning Editor** Paula Hardy **Coordinating Editor** Alison Ridgway **Coordinating Cartographers** Matthew Kelly, Csanad Csutoros **Layout Designer** Jessica Rose **Assisting Editors** Sarah Stewart, Kate Cody **Managing Cartographer** Mark Griffiths **Cover Designer** Mary Nelson-Parker **Project Managers** Fabrice Rocher **Managing Editor** Brigitte Ellemor **Mapping Development** Paul Piaia **Thanks to** Glenn Beanland, Sin Choo, Sally Darmody, Stefanie Di Trocchio, Ryan Evans, Quentin Frayne, Jennifer Garrett, Mark Germanchis, Nancy Ianni, Laura Jane, Marina Kosmatos, Darren O'Connell, Lyahna Spencer, Celia Wood, Wendy Wright

Photographs by Lonely Planet Images and Martin Moos except for the following: p36 Glenn Beanland; p8, p27 & p73 Jon Davison; p52 & p61 Dallas Stribley; p66 Thomas Winz. **Cover photograph** Display of gloves in a shop on the Via dell Spiga, Milan, Ray Roberts/Photolibrary. All images are copyright of the photographers unless otherwise indicated. Many of the images in this guide are available for licensing from Lonely Planet Images: www.lonelyplanetimages.com.

ISBN 978 1 74059 759 3

Printed through Colorcraft Ltd, Hong Kong.
Printed in China

Acknowledgments © Azienda Transporti Milanesi 2006

Contents

From the Publisher

AUTHOR
Alison Bing

Tae kwon do took Alison to Italy, but not in an Olympic kind of way. She never made it past those consolation-prize yellow belts, but she did spar with this Roman guy a few times and suddenly she was on a meet-the-parents trip to Trastevere. Twelve years and about 4015 plates of pasta later, she's ready for her purple belt in la dolce vita (as long as it doesn't clash with her shoes). Alison holds a BA in Art History from Haverford College and a masters degree from the Fletcher School of Law and Diplomacy, a joint programme of Tufts and Harvard Universities – perfectly respectable diplomatic credentials she regularly undermines with opinionated culture commentary for newspapers, magazines and radio.

Mille grazie e tanti baci a:

I cognoscenti insuperabile di Milano: Claudio Bonoldi, Elisa Bartoccini, Ilaria Ventriglia, Rosella Ghezzi, Antonio Dalle Rive e Barbara Pietrasanta (e certo Giulia)

Le mie famiglie a Roma & Stateside: the Bings, Ferrys, and Marinuccis

My posse in New York: Fabrizio ed Anais

SF: Chad Jennings & Yosh Han (perfumer and fellow traveller extraordinaire)

My editorial co-conspirators in London: Paula Hardy and Stef di Trocchio

The Melbourne mavens: Alison Ridgway, Mark Griffiths and the best cartos in the biz

Ma sopra tutto: Marco Flavio Marinucci, for taking that flying leap with me 12 years ago and every day since.

LONELY PLANET AUTHORS

Why is our travel information the best in the world? It's simple: our authors are independent, dedicated travellers. They don't research using just the Internet or phone, and they don't take freebies in exchange for positive coverage. They travel widely, to all the popular spots and off the beaten track. They personally visit thousands of hotels, restaurants, cafés, bars, galleries, palaces, museums and more – and they take pride in getting all the details right, and telling it how it is. For more, see the authors section on **www.lonelyplanet.com**.

PHOTOGRAPHER
Martin Moos

Born in Zürich, Switzerland, Martin got the obvious banking degree before escaping onto the travellers' trail with his Nikon gear in 1986. Seven years in northeast Asia provided oodles of motives for an in-depth learning-by-doing. Martin is presently based again in Zürich, together with his wife and two children, cramped by mountains of slides.

SEND US YOUR FEEDBACK

We love to hear from travellers – your comments keep us on our toes and help make our books better. Our well-travelled team reads every word on what you loved or loathed about this book. Although we cannot reply individually to postal submissions, we always guarantee that your feedback goes straight to the appropriate authors, in time for the next edition – and the most useful submissions are rewarded with a free book. To send us your updates – and find out about Lonely Planet events, newsletters and travel news – visit our award-winning website: **www.lonelyplanet.com/feedback**.

Note: We may edit, reproduce and incorporate your comments in Lonely Planet products such as guidebooks, websites and digital products, so let us know if you don't want your comments reproduced or your name acknowledged. For a copy of our privacy policy visit **www.lonelyplanet.com/privacy**.

Introducing Milan

The now and the next are invented daily in Milan, Europe's creative capital. Until Milan led the way, who knew that happy hour could last four hours, that clothing and household appliances could be made out of basketry, and that coffee could make a delicious pasta sauce? Thinking big comes with the territory here: when Leonardo da Vinci suggested canal locks might help move marble upstream to build the cathedral, Milan made it happen – and today the Duomo remains a spectacular monument to the staying power of a truly great notion.

Milan has a history of being open to outlandish ideas, some of them positively brilliant (La Scala opera openings, Milan Fashion Week, winning goals from AC Milan and Inter, the International Furniture Fair, three-hour happy hours) and others less so (Fascism, corruption scandals, Berlusconi, Italian MTV, industrial sprawl). But pointing out missteps is missing the point here – the city makes no secret of its shortcomings and finds in them inspiration for constant reinvention and redemption. When Rome fell, it crumbled; but whenever Milan stumbles in its stilettoes, it simply brings back flats.

Decadence seems practical in a city where people think hard enough to really need nights out at fabulous fusion restaurants and dance-'til-dawn clubs, and leisurely days in the park devouring gelato or at the spa sipping Franciacorta DOCG (Lombardy's best bubbly). There's no point begrudging Milanese such pleasures, because they're perfectly willing to let you join in. No need to bother about what to wear either: Milan will take care of that. Just come as you are and you're set for grand old times, fashioned into something entirely new.

Cosmopolitan Milan buzzes with energy at any time of the day

Neighbourhoods

CENTRE

Historically speaking, the centre of Milan is where all of the action is. The Duomo, La Scala, Galleria Vittorio Emanuele II, Santa Maria presso San Satiro and the Biblioteca Ambrosiana are all found in the heart of the city, in more ways than one. Hotels, restaurants and cafés cluster nearby and while most charge a premium for their primo location, some are worth it – namely Cracco-Peck, Park Hyatt Milano and Zucca in Galleria. To the north of the city is the legendary **Quadrilatero d'Oro**, the spiritual home of fashionistas worldwide – streets here are lined with designer window displays that are altars to glamour. Northwest is **Brera**, with cobblestone streets, low stucco buildings, artisans' boutiques and sidewalk cafés reminding you what old-world Italian charm is all about, and the Pinacoteca di Brera packed to the brim with Renaissance treasures.

Head to Corso Como for shopping and aperitivi

NORTH

Greenery, galleries, Art Nouveau buildings and exciting nightlife await discovery north of the city's historic centre. To the northeast you can while away afternoons in the **Giardini Pubblici** with a double dose of culture at Galleria d'Arte Moderna and Padiglione d'Arte Contemporanea (PAC), then go for a film at Spazio Oberdan. Afterwards stroll over to the magnificent Liberty (Art Nouveau) buildings for aperitivi in the Diana Garden bar. Further northeast is the **Stazione Centrale** and many of the city's most reasonably priced accommodation. Hedonists heed the siren call to the northwest in **Moscova** and **Corso Como**, for shopping, aperitivi and clubbing until dawn. Artists, activists and adventurous diners converge nightly in **Isola** for fantastic food in like-minded company.

SOUTH

Milan was once as defined by its canals as Venice, and **Navigli** offers a taste of Milanese life in the Middle Ages – only with much better food. Designers and artists are taking over the old warehouses here, and emerging designers are clustered in **Zona Tortona**, just over Graffiti Bridge from Porta Genova. Stroll **Alzaia Naviglio Grande** and **Ripa di Porta Ticinese** during the day for antiques shops and at night for pizzerias and bars. Hip shopping strip **Corso di Porta Ticinese** is just to the northeast, flanked on one side by the sombre ecclesiastical splendours of Museo Diocesano, Sant'Eustorgio and San Lorenzo alle Colonne. To the east is **Porta Romana**, with Italian design headquarters, the Fondazione Prada, and reasonably priced restaurants along tree-lined streets.

WEST

Whole days could be spent at the **Castello Sforzesco** and **Parco Sempione** without running out of things to do: dig into design at the Triennale, take in amazing views at Torre Branca, wander the Castello grounds and its ten museums, and spend happy hours at aperitivi bars around **Piazza Sempione**.

Stylish towers of Castello Sforzesco

Head to Chinatown on **Via Paolo Sarpi**, and onward to **Via Piero della Francesca** to break in those new shoes on the dance floor. To the southwest of the Castello is the smudged but still stupendous *Il Cenacolo* (The Last Supper), and further south are two monuments to Milan's religious belief and restless ingenuity: Sant'Ambrogio and Museo Nazionale della Scienza e Tecnica.

OFF THE BEATEN TRACK

Head to Milan's outer fringe and discover the hip art scene in **Lambrate** (p23), cross over to **Isola** for aperitivi with the alternative set, or cross the Graffiti Bridge to **Zona Tortona** for one-of-a-kind ensembles by emerging Milanese designers.

Itineraries

LA BELLA FIGURA

The Italian *'fare la bella figure'* means cutting a fine figure, and that's what you'll be doing as you stroll through ever-fashionable Galleria Vittorio Emanuele II (p20), with pit stops at Zucca in Galleria or Gucci Café (p57) for espresso and brioche, Piumelli Guanti (p45) for gloves and Borsalino (p46) for a hat to tip at Leonardo da Vinci's monument as you head through Piazza della Scala. Take Via Brera

Get tied up in Galleria Vittorio Emanuele II

to Pinacoteca di Brera (p11) to soak up a little Renaissance refinement, then onward to Via Solferino and Le Solferine (p44) for artisan-made footwear. Those boots were made for walking up Via Statuto to Corso Como, where you'll stop for baked goods at Princi (p54) so that you don't get too giddy shopping for Como silk at Telerie Roberto (p45) and 10 Corso Como (p46) – or its outlet around the corner (no-one will be the wiser). With your newfound Milan style, you're bound to impress the bouncers at Gasoline, Light or Hollywood (p64).

L'ARCHITETTURA

The Duomo (p10) is the main point of architectural reference in Milan, and it should be yours too: head to the roof for a tête-à-tête with the saints atop the cathedral spires. Take in the variety of architecture around the Duomo: the neoclassical glass Galleria Vittorio Emanuele II (a major inspiration for Massimiliano Fuksas's new glass Feria), the stone cold Fascist Palazzo dell'Arengario, the gone-for-baroque interiors at the Palazzo Reale. Detour through the arcaded Palazzo Ragione (p27) for pure

Sunlight illuminates the heavens inside the Duomo

Aperitivo alfresco down Corso di Porta Ticinese

medieval charm and stop at the pinkish Italian Bar (p53) to enjoy lunch and its perennially rosy outlook. Walk along Via Spadari past the elegant Liberty (Art Nouveau) building façades on your way to Santa Maria presso San Satiro (p15), the Renaissance showstopper with Bramante's spatial effects. Skirt the southern wall of the Duomo to reach Corso Europa and Via Durini, where interior architecture and design showplaces (p24) conspire to convince you that you need a chaise longue in your bathroom. Literally bathe in architectural splendour at Gianfranco Ferre E'Spa (p30), where eye-popping gold mosaics help keep you from falling asleep in the hot tub.

LA DOLCE VITA

Life is sweet as you take a wander through Parco Sempione (p29), checking out the latest in art and design at the Triennale (p23) and its Design Caffé, taking in the view atop Torre Branca (p28), and strolling the grounds of the Castello Sforzesco (p19) like you owned the place. You're in for a royal treat at the Luini fresco-covered royal chapel at San Maurizio (p29), followed by another at Chocolat (p58). It would be sweet indeed if you managed to get tickets to see *Il Cenacolo* (p13) nearby, but otherwise you can enjoy some people-watching at Bar Magenta (p62) before you head down the street to discover the effortless elegance of Sant'Ambrogio (p16). Enjoy a happy hour or three at Le Biciclette (p61) – ahh, this is the life!

LOWLIGHTS

- *Zanzara*: 'mosquito' sounds funny in Italian, but on summer nights in Navigli, it's no joke.
- Concrete jungle: looks like somebody was in a rush to build after the war... good thing Milan is hiring better architects these days.
- Freak hailstorms: guess you won't be going out tonight after all. On the bright side, wait until you see how blue the sky is tomorrow morning.
- McDonald's: more of them here than in any other city in Italy and all of them totally unnecessary – Milan's meat-stuffed *panini* (grilled sandwiches) are the stuff of legend.

DUOMO (3, D5)

This marvel in marble took six centuries to create and may take another six to comprehend. Gian Galeazzo Visconti had grand designs on the city in 1387, and rallied support for a massive new Duomo. To win over naysayers, he agreed to cover the cost of the lavish pinkish-grey **Candoglia marble**.

As the edifice went up, objections were raised. Engineers denounced the massive structure as unscientific and unconstructable. The marble was nice, but how could the largest slabs be transported through the narrow streets to the centre? The Duomo's last-mile problem was solved by Leonardo da Vinci, whose **canal lock** mechanism raised water levels one canal section at a time, all the way to the Duomo (see p17). As always in Milan, there was also the matter of style. By the time the cathedral began taking shape, the rest of Italy had moved on from French-inspired Gothic and even resented its intrusion, along with Napoleonic conquests of Northern Italy.

But rather than stripping away Gothic ornament, Milan piled it on, hiring Italian stonemasons and sculptors to literally take Gothic to the next level with **spires** capped by **thousands of sculptures** in a fusion International High Gothic style. But don't be surprised if some of its splendours are under wraps when you visit – like certain ladies who lunch in the Quadrilatero d'Oro, the Duomo gets a little work done to its face and backside on a regular basis.

INFORMATION

- ✉ Piazza del Duomo
- € Duomo free, Battistero di San Giovanni €1.50, stairs to roof €3.50, lift €5
- 🕓 Duomo 7am-7pm, Battistero di San Giovanni 9.45am-12.45pm & 2.45-5.45pm Tue-Sun, roof 9am-5.45pm, lift 9am-5.30pm
- ♿ ramps to entrance of cathedral only
- M Duomo
- ✕ Luini (p53)

DON'T MISS

- Being on top of the world with the gargoyles on the roof terrace
- The *ascensore* (lift) to the roof – saves 150 steps and a whole lot of breath
- Video art in the crypt: Mark Wallinger blocks out all but the edges of the Zefirelli film *Via Dolorosa*, in a computer-crash crisis of faith

Breathtaking views of Duomo's rooftop spires

PINACOTECA DI BRERA (3, C1)

To imagine the ingenuity of the Renaissance, you kind of had to be there – and at the Pinacoteca di Brera, you can be. Stroll through frozen medieval tableaux produced in anonymous workshops, and suddenly you'll leap forward into relatable human dramas by painters known by name, from the revolutions of Raphael, Mantegna, and Piero della Francesca to the refinements of Titian, Caravaggio, and Tintoretto.

The Pinacoteca was established in 1809 with paintings from religious institutions Napoleon had, erm, borrowed for safekeeping, and bequests amassed even more works on religious themes. Today the collection reveals how different artists handled the same story at different times in history, with social issues of the day and psychological concerns of the moment finding their way into the painting through the artist's brush. Compare **Veronese's Last Supper** here to Leonardo's **Il Cenacolo** (p13), and you'll notice the apostles are running amok in Veronese's work, distracted from Jesus by food, wine and a begging dog. Veronese was reprimanded by the Inquisition authorities for this radical interpretation, but he refused to change it under threat of imprisonment. Finally the work was retitled *Dinner in the House of Levi,* and the Inquisition let it slide in a landmark victory for Renaissance creative freedom.

INFORMATION

- ☎ 02 722 631
- 🖳 www.brera.beniculturali.it
- ✉ Palazzo di Brera, Via Brera 28
- € €5/2.50
- 🕑 8.30am-7.15pm Tue-Sun
- ℹ audio guide €3.50
- Ⓜ Lanza
- ♿ excellent
- 🍴 Bar Jamaica (p52)

DON'T MISS

- Brera Mai Vista (Never Seen in Brera) exhibits reveal hidden gems and newly restored works, so you never know what'll go into rotation tomorrow…think they'd notice if you set up camp in the courtyard?
- Caravaggio's *Cena in Emmaus*, where a simple meal turns into a blessed event – something every foodie in Italy can relate to
- Francesco Hayez' *Il Bacio*, romance Italian-style, with a big smooch and a snappy feathered cap that could make a comeback next season

LA SCALA (3, C3)

Until the mid-20th century, even Italy's most celebrated divas were scared to perform here for fear of the *fischi* (taunting whistles) from the **loggione**, opera's toughest critics in La Scala's upper **loggie**. But if whistling seems rude, you should have been here during the heyday of Rossini and Verdi in the 18th and 19th centuries, when audience members gambled, chatted and walked in and out during shows, their enormous hats and wigs blotting out the stage.

INFORMATION

- ☎ 02 861 778
  (reservation confirmation line)
- 🖥 www.teatroallascala.org
- ✉ Piazza della Scala
- ☼ 8.30am-7.15pm Tue-Sun
- ⓘ 02 720 03 744 (information line)
- Ⓜ Duomo
- ♿ access available
- ✖ Don Carlos (p51)

DON'T MISS

- Seeing a performance here – any performance, really
- Early reviews from loggione at intermission
- The glorious central chandelier (not that you could miss it)
- La Scala Museo Teatrale (p22)

All that would change under Arturo Toscanini, La Scala's conductor from 1898 to 1929, who insisted that operas should be about music. He dimmed the lights to focus audience attention on-stage, installed the **golfo mistico** (orchestra pit), and stormed out when an audience demanded an encore and broke the orchestra's momentum. He also had no patience for Fascism, and resigned his post and left the country rather than play along to Mussolini's tune. But after WWII bombing raids destroyed the theatre, he raised funds to rebuild La Scala, and performed at its 1946 reopening.

La Scala was overhauled and reopened in 2004, with a controversial new **round wing** by modernist Mario Botta that's almost disappointingly inoffensive, even dull. But La Scala continues to take risks: a musicians' mutiny recently ousted Riccardo Muti as the conductor, and new guest conductor Daniel Barenboim's first season included an orchestra of musicians from Israel, the Palestinian Territories and other Middle Eastern countries.

Leonardo da Vinci watches over La Scala

IL CENACOLO (THE LAST SUPPER) (2, B4)

Take a long, hard squint, because despite the best efforts of restorers, one of the world's masterpieces is gradually fading. In 1495, Leonardo da Vinci was commissioned to paint the back wall of the **Santa Maria delle Grazie** convent dining hall by Ludovico Sforza, whose wife Beatrice d'Este was a major supporter of Leonardo's work despite his unconventional methods. Sometimes he wouldn't pick up a brush for days, and then in a single day he'd cover large sections, as though taking dictation from a dream. Instead of painting the apostles demurely facing forward, Leonardo imagined each apostle reacting dramatically to Jesus' revelation: 'One of you will betray me'. He painted tempera directly on the wall, not atop wet fresco plaster that might slow him down or dull his colours. Four years later, no one could argue with the results: brilliant colour, palpable emotion, and instead of haloes, a suffused light that seems to come from within.

The downside of Leonardo's revolutionary approach soon became apparent in Milan's damp winters, when the paint started to flake off the plaster. French troops quartered in the convent in the 16th and 18th weren't exactly tidy, and when restorers later tried to remove all that soot and grime with cotton and alcohol, they inadvertently lifted a layer of Leonardo's paint. The mural was miraculously left standing when the refectory was bombed in WWII, but further damage was done.

But while time is erasing details of the apostle's facial expressions, you can still read their reactions in their position and movements – the ancient mural is becoming an abstract modern painting, pure composition and expression. Leonardo da Vinci's challenge was to picture belief rising above betrayal; ours is to perceive it despite the effects of disaster, war and human error.

INFORMATION

- ☎ 02 894 21 146
- 💻 www.cenacolovinciano.it
- ✉ Piazza Santa Maria delle Grazie 2, Corso Magenta
- € €6.50/free plus booking fee €1.50 per person
- ☽ 8.15am-6.45pm Tue-Sun
- ⓘ audioguide per person €3.25
- Ⓜ Cadorna, Conciliazione
- ♿ access available
- ✕ Noy (p61)

DON'T MISS

- Your ticket: call at least a week or two ahead for a time slot and reservation number. Show up 30 minutes before to claim your ticket, or it'll be resold.
- Jesus' feet: no, this isn't a *Da Vinci Code* conspiracy – they were cut off when the floor was raised in the 17th century.
- The sublime dimensions and spectacular paintings of Santa Maria delle Grazie next door

QUADRILATERO D'ORO (3, E2)

You don't have to be a big spender to get giddy in the 'Golden Quad' – you'll get a retail buzz just window shopping along **Via della Spiga** (north), **Via Sant'Andrea** (east), **Via Monte Napoleone** (south) and **Via Alessandro Manzoni** (west). Shopping is actually a secondary pastime in the Quad: the first and most important is strutting. Have an espresso or spumante at **Caffé Cova** (p57) or **Emporio Armani Caffé** (p52) and watch the parade go by: playboys with Fendi shades mysteriously suspended mid-forehead, models in sensible shoes and swinging ponytails, fashion designers sporting fabric swatches as scarves.

An afternoon among the glitterati in the Quad could leave you a little Midas-touched in the head: you may have to go into glitz-detox. Beat a hasty retreat from the logo-mad masses to the **Museo Bagatti Valsecchi** for Renaissance splendour, or head to **PAC** (p22) for contemporary art minus the commercial overtones. When your tootsies are tired, give them some downtime at **Dolce & Gabbana's Beauty Farm** (p30), or slip into the metallic hot tub at **ESPA at Gianfranco Ferré** (p30) before you try those **Prada** heels or **Zegna** suits.

INFORMATION

- ✉ bordered by Via della Spiga, Via Sant'Andrea, Via Monte Napoleone & Via Alessandro Manzoni
- ☽ shops generally open 10am-7pm Mon-Sat (some open at 3pm Mon)
- Ⓜ Montenapoleone/San Babila
- ♿ footpaths are narrow, but shops are street level; some cobblestones
- ✕ Paper Moon (p53)

DON'T MISS

- Milan's January and July sales, if you dare – only the strong survive
- Designer row Via Durini to the southwest of the Quad, to find the perfect couch to match your Pucci outfit
- San Francesco di Paola (p28), the gilt-bedecked baroque church that puts the sparkle in the quad
- Lunching among the ladies who do it professionally at Il Salumaio (p52) or Bagutta (p54).

Get that retail buzz along Via della Spiga

SANTA MARIA PRESSO SAN SATIRO (3, C5)

The **Romanesque brick exterior** of the biggest little church in Milan has the charms of a medieval castle – but in no way does it prepare you for the Renaissance splendours that you will see when you step inside its impressive façade. Ludovico Sforza saw potential in this little church built on top of the 9th-century mausoleum of martyr San Satiro, and asked architect Donato Bramante to spruce up the place in 1482. Bramante was not about to allow any space limitations to cramp his style: he painted a **trompe-l'oeil coffered niche** on the shallow apse, which made the simple backdrop to the altar look like the magnificent Pantheon in Rome.

The Renaissance dome of the small church also shed new light on the ancient **Sacello di San Satiro** as well as its early Christian frescoes, classical columns and mythical beasts. The sacred **Madonna with Child** which resides over the altar is another relic from an earlier, more pugnacious time: it hung outside the Sacello di San Satiro until some young men were stabbed in a street fight in front of the building, and the painting began to weep blood. Multitudes congregated outside the church to witness the miracle, until the painting was finally brought inside the church where it could be worshipped by masses without causing yet another traffic jam in Milan.

INFORMATION

✉ Via Torino at Via Speronari

🕒 7.30-11.30am, 3-7pm Mon-Fri; 9.30-11.30am, 3-7pm Sat; 8.30am-12.30pm, 3-7pm Sun

Ⓜ Duomo

♿ access available

DON'T MISS

- The sacristy done in Bramante's style, with a tiny octagonal dome surrounded by flocks of terracotta angels.
- Renaissance roundel windows that fill the church transept with otherworldly light and seem to raise the vaulted ceilings.
- Afternoon organ concerts – check the bulletin board near the door for times.

BASILICA DI SANT'AMBROGIO (2, B4)

Milan's patron saint Ambrogio rose to power rather suddenly, graduating from public servant to bishop in about a week after rowdy Milanese crowds demanded his appointment. Sant'Ambrogio proved to be a quick study and unusually gutsy, a staunch defender of the poor and opponent of Arianism, Lombardy's main religion at the time. For all his successful politicking, he wouldn't sacrifice principle for diplomacy – he demanded that Emperor Theodosius repent for the massacre of 7,000 people at Thessolonica under threat of excommunication. After Ambroggio's death in AD 397, his body was entombed at this church named for him, where it can be viewed today in spooky desiccated form.

The church itself is a more fitting legacy: the solid brick structure is well grounded, and its purposeful simplicity is truly uplifting. Walk into the arcaded courtyard, and the front of the church rises majestically in front of you, one row of arches carefully balanced atop another to reach right up to the gabled roof. Once inside, your eye may be caught by the shimmering **altar mosaics** and AD 835 **gilt altarpiece** telling Sant'Ambrogio's life story – but wait 'til you see the 4th to 6th century mosaics inside the **Sacello San Vittore** in **Ciel d'Oro**, its 'golden sky' dome supported by winged monkeys and griffins.

INFORMATION

- ☎ 02 864 50 895
- ✉ Piazza Sant'Ambrogio 15
- ☽ Basilica 7am-noon & 2-7pm Mon-Sat, 7am-1.15pm & 2.30-7.45pm Sun; Museum 10am-noon & 3-5pm Wed-Fri & Mon, 3-5pm Sat & Sun
- Ⓜ Sant'Ambrogio
- ✗ Le Biciclette (p61)

DON'T MISS

- Donato Bramante's cloisters at the adjoining Università Cattolica del Sacro Cuore (1497–1513), painstakingly restored to their original design after WWII bombing
- Bernardino Luini's painting of the four evangelists surrounded by cherubs watching them expectantly, like kids awaiting a bedtime story
- Giambattista Tiepolo's action-packed *Shipwreck of San Satiro*, with an angel appearing on a cresting wave like a holy surfer

Exquisite craftsmanship on the pulpit in Basilica di Sant'Ambrogio

NAVIGLI (2, B6)

Picturesque as they are, Milan's Navigli (canals) were also practical solutions to economic and artistic problems for medieval Milan. Food and wine had to be brought to town somehow – Milanese were known to riot when their wine supply was cut off – and luckily there were tributaries on the surrounding river plains that could be diverted for use as canals.

The Navigli Grande started life as a humble medieval irrigation ditch in 1171, and over the course of 100 years became a thoroughfare for essentials like salt, cheese, wine, and manure (not necessarily all on the same boatload). More canals were constructed in concentric rings around Milan to transport marble to build the **Duomo** (p10), though most have since been filled to serve as Milan's major ring-road thoroughfares.

The Navigli neighbourhood (named after its major feature) was once marshland, and might return to its natural state if not for ingenious pumps and dredging systems credited to (who else?) Leonardo da Vinci – too bad he couldn't devise coping mechanisms for Navigli's notorious mosquitoes in summer. But bug spray is a minor inconvenience for the privilege of roaming around Navigli on a hot summer's evening, when the streets are closed to traffic, **El Brellin** (p61) is serving aperitivi canalside, and restaurants like **Le Vigne** (p56) and **Sadler** (p56) are dishing out some of Milan's finest food and drink – no need to run riot.

INFORMATION

- ☽ late afternoon until late at night
- ♿ difficult; can only traverse canals at Darsena
- Ⓜ Porta Garibaldi
- ✖ Le Vigne (p56)

DON'T MISS

- Mercatone Antiquario: on the last Sunday of every month, attracts antique dealers from across Northern Italy
- Zona Tortona: the former warehouse district along Vias Tortona and Savona, repurposed as artisans' studios and designer outlets
- Zanelotti Salami: maintaining Milan's reputation for cold cuts with hand-cranked equipment, one link at a time

BIBLIOTECA AMBROSIANA (3, B5)

When the bookish young cardinal Federico Borromeo built the Biblioteca Ambrosiana in 1609, the building was much more than **Europe's first public library**. To get any reading or study done here back then, you would have had to shush the hordes of artists, writers and philosophers who converged on this building to chat, debate and pontificate. Schools for writing and fine arts flourished on the premises, and Borromeo even put his own collection of artworks up for discussion on the first floor of the building.

INFORMATION

- ☎ 02 80 69 21
- 🖥 www.ambrosiana.it
- ✉ Piazza Pio XI 2
- € €7.50/4.50
- 🕙 10am-5.30pm Tue-Sun
- Ⓜ Duomo, Cordusio
- ♿ good; stair lift to the entrance
- ✗ Italian Bar (p53)

The library on the ground floor expanded to include 75,000 volumes and 35,000 manuscripts –including ones that Leonardo da Vinci famously wrote in cryptic mirror-image script. Meanwhile the art collection housed upstairs took historic shape with breakthrough works of art like Rembrandt's face-pulling self-portraits, Caravaggio's *Canestra di Frutta* (Basket of Fruit) that initiated Italy's still-life painting tradition, and Bernardino Luini's charming *Holy Family*: plump, smiling and apparently boneless.

DON'T MISS

- Your chance to make like a Renaissance scholar and research the topic of your choice – sign up using the computers at the entry (from 9.30am to 5pm Monday to Friday)
- Models of Leonardo's designs from his Atlantic Codex

Biblioteca Ambrosiana: Europe's first public library and 17th-century artists' centre

CASTELLO SFORZESCO (2, C3)

Back in Italian city-state days, you never knew when dignitaries might decide to take over while they were visiting – hence the popularity of castle strongholds. As a major centre for trade, Milan had many assets to protect, and built the Castello Sforzesco in grand style and scale to let outsiders know it meant business. Galeazzo Visconti got it started in 1368, but it was torn down by masses when they ousted the Viscontis in 1447, and the stones were used to build city walls. The building was re-styled from a fortress to a palace under the Sforzas with the help of da Vinci and Bramante, who probably built the **Ponticella** (bridge) over the moat. The Sforzas were more interested in architecture and sports than creature comforts: their first order was the elaborate arcaded **Rochetta** with a court for playing a game like tennis, and they only moved out of their modest rooms by the henhouse once the **Ducal Court** was built.

INFORMATION

- ☎ 02 884 63 700
- 🖳 www.milano castello.it
- ✉ Piazza Castello
- € free
- 🕓 9am-5.30pm
- Ⓜ Caroli, Cadorna, Lanza
- ♿ some rooms accessible
- ✗ La Brisa (p58)

But even with defences devised by Leonardo, the castle couldn't keep out the wily French, or the waves of plague that killed 80,000 Milanese between 1524 and 1528. Troops and horses were quartered in the Castello by the French, then the Spanish, and the Austrians after them. Napoleon had grand plans to develop the place, but he was ousted in 1815 before they could materialize. The Castello became a focal point for Milanese resentment against Austrians, who used its **secret passageways** to hide out during Milan's five-day uprising in 1848. Men and women who rebelled against Austrian authority were buried under the castle, until a unified Italy finally ousted the Habsburgs. Local architect Luca Beltrami undertook a controversial restoration that added new details like the massive **round towers**, and exposed frescos and other authentic details from an earlier time.

DON'T MISS

- The starry-skied Capella Ducale, from the stellar glory days of Bramante and da Vinci
- A stroll in Parco Sempione (p29) – and maybe an aperitivo at Bar Bianco (p65)
- The Mango Longo in the Museum of Musical Instruments – a white-striped, mango-shaped guitar you wouldn't dream about smashing

Beltrami's new/old Castello was conceived not as a fortification but as a showcase for Milan's true strength: creativity. No less than 10 museums are housed here, including these standouts:

Achille Bertarelli Prints Collection Giant ancient maps, engraved postcards, opera fans, and other ephemera from Milan's extraordinary paper trail.

Museo d'Arte Antica Lombard statuary is the focus here, with very noteworthy exceptions: Michelangelo's unfinished final work, *Rondanini Pietà,* which he apparently worked on right up until his death in 1564, and a fresco widely attributed to Leonardo da Vinci, *Sala delle Asse* (1498) in Room 8.

Museum of Musical Instruments A quirky collection with some of the world's first (and screechiest) violins, hurdy-gurdys and a double virginal piano built to be played by two (no double entendre intended).

Photographic Archive 600,000 photos trace Italy's early history of photography back to 1840, from experimental daguerreotypes to 1898 documentary footage of Milan's workers' strikes.

Pinacoteca Artists from Lombardy are the strength of this collection, especially Vincenzo Foppa's Lombard Renaissance masterwork, *Madonna of the Golden Book*, showing a blushing Madonna and baby surrounded by staring angels and songbirds in apple trees.

GALLERIA VITTORIO EMANUELE II (3, C4)

Just steps away from the Duomo is the grand entry to Milan's other precocious feat of engineering, and this one's specially designed to leave your wallet a bit lighter. The Galleria was conceived as a showplace for modern Milan by Giuseppe Mengoni, who plummeted to his death on the job in 1877, just before his 14-year pet project was finally complete. To avoid such luck, it couldn't hurt to observe Milanese tradition: head under the vast **glass dome** to the **mosaic of the bull** on the floor, and grind your heel firmly into its testicles. Recently the bull has been covered to protect it from the ravages of stilettos – but word is the bull and its equipment will be back in service soon.

You may need the determination of a bull to emerge from the Galleria without a shopping bag from one of the many retail sirens lining the Gallery, including a small luggage shop that's now described in hushed tones as the **original Prada store**. But even though a McDonald's sneaked in among the cafés and under the radar of Milan's city council (tsk, tsk), this is no ordinary mall. The shattered glass was replaced after WWII, but this is essentially the same lofty neoclassical structure that has served as a triumphal arch for successful shoppers for over a century.

INFORMATION

- ✉ Galleria Vittorio Emanuele II
- € free
- ☽ 24hr
- Ⓜ Duomo
- ♿ ground level access
- ✕ Zucca in Galleria (p57)

DON'T MISS

- The mosaics behind the bar at Zucca in Galleria (p57)
- Advertising that melts in your mouth: logo chocolates from Gucci Caffé (p57)
- The woozy view looking up at the dome while spinning on the bull

Sights & Activities

MUSEUMS, GALLERIES & SHOWROOMS

Museums

Casa Museo Boschi di Stefano (2, E2)
The next best thing to inheriting a wealthy, eccentric Milanese great-grandmother's art collection is visiting this charming flat packed with 300 paintings by 20th-century greats. Imagine the salon conversations started here, with Paula Moderson-Becker's expressionist girl sneaking sidelong glances, Umberto Boccini's dynamic brushstrokes propelling painting towards futurism, Mario Sironi's brooding, fragmented post-war landscapes and Lucio Fontana's provocative slashed paintings.
☎ 02 202 40 568 ⊠ Via Jan 15 € free ☽ 2-6pm Wed-Sun Ⓜ Lima

Galleria d'Arte Moderna (3, F1)
Rush past the watchful eyes of Milanese neoclassical portraits and anatomically

San Siro stadium home to Inter Milan and AC Milan

correct miniatures, upstairs past medieval Madonnas and lonesome Buddhas, and emerge facing Volpedo's pointillist marching workers in *The Fourth Estate*. From here, leapfrog the French Impressionists to Giacomo Balla's futurist masterworks and Medardo Rosso's creepy, cackling wax children from the Palazzo Reale's 20th-century collection.
☎ 02 760 02 819 ⊠ Via Palestro 16 € free

☽ 9am-1pm & 2-5.30pm Tue-Sun Ⓜ Palestro

Museo Bagatti Valsecchi (3, E2)
Though born a few centuries too late, the Bagatti Valsecchi brothers were determined to be Renaissance men, and from 1878 to 1887 built their home as a living museum of the quattrocento. The dauntless interior decorators accepted no cheap reproductions, and collected authentic

GOOOOOOOAAAAAL!

Whether you're an AC Milan fan or Inter enthusiast, Milan's **San Siro Stadium** is where you want to be on a sunny Sunday afternoon, chiming in on Italy's latest favourite footie chant: 'Duh…da-dah da-dah duh, duh…' (better known as the bass line to the White Stripes song 'Seven Nation Army'). Forget parking: take the red line to Lotto and the free shuttle bus, or the red line to De Angeli and then tram 16. Afterwards, you'll be doing a 20-minute walk of shame or triumph with everyone else back to Lotto.

Here's how to score tickets, which range from €15 to €115:

AC Milan Buy online at www.acmilan.com or at any **Cariplo Bank** (3, C3; Via Verdi 8; ☽ 8.45am-1.45pm & 2.45-3.45pm Mon-Fri; Ⓜ Duomo) or **Milan Point** (Piazza XXIV Maggio, cnr Via San Gottardo; ☽ 10am-7pm Tue-Sat; Ⓜ Porta Genova).

Inter Buy online at www.inter.it or in person at any **Banca Popolare di Milano** (3, D3; Piazza Meda 4; ☽ 8.45am-1.45pm & 2.45-3.45pm Mon-Fri; Ⓜ San Babila).

and painstakingly restored period pieces – hence the throne-like chairs and bathroom crucifixion triptych. ☎ 02 760 06 132 ▯ www .museobagattivalsecchi.org ✉ Via Gesù 5 € usually €6 except Wed €3 ☽ 1-5.45pm Tue-Sun Ⓜ Montenapoleone

Museo Diocesano (2, C5)

Don't be taken in by the false modesty of these tranquil white 16th-century cloisters: Milan's archdiocese has quite a collection, and knows how to put on a show. A recent exhibit spotlighted Renaissance painter Andrea Mantegna, whose views of Jesus on the cross from the feet up established him as the reigning champion of extreme perspective. ▯ www.museodiocesano .it ✉ Corso di Porta Ticinese 95 € €6/€5 ☽ 10am-6pm Tue-Sun Ⓜ Porta Genova

Museo Inter e Milan

Cartoonish papier-mâché dummies of 24 football stars add a little light humour to this shrine of testosterone, boasting nonstop match videos and trophies galore. The accompanying stadium tour covers the locker room, where you can rest your bum on the same bench as countless naked football legends. Before any stalkerish ideas come to mind: on game day, the museum closes 30 minutes before kickoff, and tours end early. ☎ 02 404 24 32 ▯ www .sansirotour.com ✉ Via Piccolomini 5, Gate 21 ☽ 10am-5pm € €12.50 Ⓜ red line to De Angeli, then tram 16

Museo Poldi-Pezzoli (3, D3)

Bill Gates seems like a pauper once you've seen the treasure trove amassed by Giacomo Poldi-Pezzoli in 1881. Pollaiuolo's girl in pearl earrings rivals Vermeer's, easily holding her own amongst angelic-action-packed Tiepolos and Moroni's smirking knight in black. One room showcases timepieces, including one boastful watch painted with women admiring it; another chamber features chests engraved with maps showing Australia as a porcupine. ☎ 02 79 48 89 ✉ Via Alessandro Manzoni 12 € €6/4 ☽ 10am-6pm Tue-Sun Ⓜ Montenapoleone

Museo Teatrale alla Scala (3, C4)

'Untutored hands may not touch me', are the words of a true diva, inscribed here on an 18th-century *spinette* (piano). *Harlequino* costumes and playing cards left at La Scala also hint at centuries of Milanese musical drama, on and off stage. Portraits show Rossini apparently chatting up patrons, while Verdi seems troubled by mixed reviews, and Callas a goddess towering above critique. ☎ 02 469 12 49 ✉ Piazza della Scala € €5/4 ☽ 9am-6pm Tue-Sat Ⓜ Duomo

Padiglione d'Arte Contemporanea (PAC) (3, F1)

A 1993 Mafia-related bombing couldn't daunt the gutsy PAC, which arose from the ashes in true Milanese fashion to mount ever more daring shows. *LESS: Alternative Strategies for Living* challenged 18 artists to invent new habitats, and results included Vito Acconci's quixotically maternal *Adjustable Wall Bra* and Silvio Wolf's moving soundscape of recent immigrants' impressions of Milan in their native languages. ☎ 02 760 09 085 ▯ www.comune.milano .it/pac ✉ Via Palestro 14 € free, depending on exhibition ☽ 9.30am-5.30pm Tue-Fri, until 7pm Sat-Sun, closed Mon Ⓜ Palestro

Studio Museo Castiglioni (2, B4)

Discover where great Italian designs come from at the studio of the Castiglioni

Discover a treasure trove at Museo Poldi-Pezzoli

brothers, whose historic designs range from the streetlight-turned-pendulum Arco floor lamp for Flos (p26) to cheeky downward-spiralling Alessi ashtrays (see p46). See prototypes from its 1960s to '80s heyday and the objects that inspired them, including bicycle seats and toys made of Iranian beer cans.
☎ 02 72 43 41
✉ Piazza Castello 27
€ €2 ⏰ 10.30am-8.30pm Tue-Sun Ⓜ Cadorna

Triennale di Milano
(2, B3)
Aficionados of architecture, design and popular culture may have to be pried away from this place with a specially-designed crowbar. Home to the Permanent Collection of Italian Design, the Triennale also features four or five other exhibitions

at once, all ingeniously presented: floating helium speech balloons explained a recent show on comics, while Le Corbusier's prefab house was set up on the lawn.
☎ 02 724 34 212 ⌨ www .triennale.it ✉ Viale Alemanga 6 € varies, depending on exhibit
⏰ 10.30am-8.30pm Tue-Sun Ⓜ Cadorna

Galleries
Antonio Colombo Arte Contemporanea (2, C2)
While most downtown galleries bank on international blue-chip artists, this plucky upstart still gambles on emerging Italian artists – and when it works, the payoff is that much greater (and the prices are better, too). Recent finds include Andrea Mastrovito's delicately outrageous

Poster at Spazio Oberdan cinema & gallery (p24)

Dracula-meets-Batman watercolours, and Luiggi Presicce's ghoulish toys.
☎ 02 290 60 171 ✉ Via Solferino 44 ⏰ 4-7.30pm Tue-Sat Ⓜ Moscova € free

---

THE HIP GALLERY HOP TO LAMBRATE
Lately the avant-garde art scene has taken the green line metro 15 minutes from Brera's Lanza station to Lambrate. Do likewise from Tuesday to Saturday between noon and 7.30pm, pass defunct factories and new offices for design mags *Domus* and *Abitare*, and you'll find:

Francesca Minini (2, F1; ☎ 02 269 24 671; ⌨ www.francescaminini.it; Via Massimiano 25; free) Intriguing ideas, including Gabriele Pico's Fiat 500 with a cloud tied to its roof.

Galleria Klerkx (2, F1; ☎ 02 215 97 763; ⌨ www.manuelaklerkx.com; Via Massimiano 25; free) Simone Tosca's computerised wall drawings and other technology-assisted flights of fancy.

Galleria Massimo de Carlo (2, F1; ☎ 02 700 03 987; ⌨ www.massimodecarlo .it; Via Ventura 5, rear bldg; free) The sheer audacity of Assume Vivid Astro Focus' homoerotic, psychotropic mall wall decals.

Galleria Zero (2, F1; ⌨ www.galleriazero.it; Via Ventura 5, front bldg, upper level; free) Deliberate provocations like Massimo Grimaldi's smashed guitar inside a collapsed tent.

Prometeogallery (2, F1; ☎ 02 269 24 450; ⌨ www.prometeogallery.com; Via Ventura 3; free) Genuinely moving pictures, such as Gulsun Karamustafa's video diptych of riots and household routines.

Fondazione Prada (2, E5)
Big enough for a B52 or, say, a full-scale killer whale made of scavenged pieces of white foamcore by Tom Sachs, the Fondazione Prada produces two grand-scale, original solo shows each year. The Sachs show captured our touchy times with fragile giants dangerously near blunt tools, and a live-in control tower for a paranoiac complete with weather monitors, radar, guns, cigarettes and vodka.
☎ 02 546 70 216 🖳 www .fondazioneprada.org ✉ Via Andrea Maffei 2 € free
🕑 9am-7pm Mon-Fri
Ⓜ Porta Romana

Galleria Cardi & Co (2, D3)
One of Milan's best-kept secrets is on a quiet street, through the courtyard and past garage doors: a polished concrete box often filled by Italy's most polished conceptual artists. Pier Paolo Calzolari recently showed lead and copper books slowly leaking saltwater onto white table-cloths, like fountains of knowledge reduced to tears.
☎ 02 626 90 945 🖳 www .galleriacardi.com ✉ Corso di Porta Nuova 8 € free
🕑 10.30am-1.30pm & 2.30-7.30pm Tue-Sat
Ⓜ Turati

Galleria Corsoveneziaotto (3, F3)
Facelifts are unnecessary in Milan, because this gallery keeps eyebrows perma-nently up with sensations like Wim Delvoye's recent showcase of Milan's favour-ite media: pork. One whiff of his exquisite inlaid floor reveals that it was made entirely of Milanese salami, and taxidermied pigs tattooed with Louis Vuitton logos seem tailor-made to scandalise fashion-conscious Milan.
☎ 02 365 05 481
✉ Corso Venezia 8 € free
🕑 10.00am-1pm & 3.30-7.30pm Mon-Fri Ⓜ Porta Venezia

Galleria Milano (2, D3)
There is no beauty without risk, as this modern gallery in a historic palazzo has proved for decades. The vaulted ceiling of the grand salon was recently repainted with what looked like heraldic patterns from afar, but on closer inspection turned out to be thousands of mosquitoes hand-drawn by contemporary artist Vincenzo Agnetti.
☎ 02 290 00 352 🖳 www .galleriamilano.com ✉ Via Manin 13 (at Via Turati)
€ free 🕑 10.00am-1pm & 4-8pm Tue-Sat Ⓜ Turati

Photology (2, C3)
Tear yourself away from the gorgeous photography catalogues in the storefront bookstore and check out the gallery out back in the garden shed, where those *X Portfolio* fetish shots that got Robert Mapplethorpe censored in the US recently shared wall space with bored nudes in mod wigs by Andy Warhol and Carlo Mollino.
☎ 02 659 52 85 🖳 www .photology.com ✉ Via della Moscova 25 € free
🕑 11am-7pm Tue-Sat
Ⓜ Moscova

Spazio Oberdan (2, E3)
Art-house cinema down-stairs, art gallery upstairs: Spazio Oberdan is artistically ambidextrous, with video art to bridge the two. Ambi-tious programs include *Ecce Uomo*, a show of blockbuster artists feeling Jesus' pain, from Damien Hirst's wry *Dead Ends* – a medicine cabinet full of cigarette butts smoked religiously – to William Kentridge's animated waves of grief in *Tide Table*.
☎ 02 774 06 300 ✉ Viale Vittorio Veneto 2 € €6
🕑 10am-7.30pm Tue-Sun
Ⓜ Porta Venezia

Design Showrooms
Artemide (3,D3)
Aesthetically inclined genies everywhere would like to announce that they're done with the whole brass oil-lamp schtick, and would appreciate if you'd rub on an Artemide next time you want a wish granted. Giancarlo Matteoli's 1965 blue mushroom-shaped Nesso table lamp would be ideal, and the Dalú transpar-ent orange plastic study light shaped like hoodie sweatshirt would suit a smallish sprite.
☎ 02 778 71 22 01
🖳 www.artemide.com
✉ Via Manzoni 12
🕑 10am-7pm Tue-Sat
Ⓜ Montenapoleone

Bisazza (3, F3)
The first and last name in modern mosaics has opened a Milan showroom where tiny tesserae get together and stage riots of colour and pattern, then mysteriously

Get minimalist at B&B Italia Store

cohere into a fluttering kelp forest, or luminous jellyfish trailing tentacles like royal trains.

☎ 02 760 21 313 ✉ Via Senato 2 🕑 10am-7pm Tue-Sat Ⓜ San Babila

B&B Italia Store (3, F5)
Mood lighting hardly seems necessary when you've got an effortlessly handsome, reclining, whisper-soft grey sofa inviting you to relax and stay awhile. A giant foot end table with upturned toes and bean-bag coffee tables that take after 1950s ashtrays hint that this dashing minimalist brand has a sense of humour, too…could this be love?

☎ 02 76 44 41 ✉ 14 Via Durini 🕑 10am-7pm Tue-Sat, 3-7pm Mon Ⓜ San Babila

Cassina (3, F5)
The latest low chairs are accessibly priced, too, without stinting on ultramodern details: snazzy wool weave and organic shapes in sunset colours, with outstitching highlighting those fluid lines. Practical issues involving suitcases may momentarily prevail, but the same thought eventually occurs to every design-driven traveller who sees Gió Ponti's 1955 classic *superleggera* (superlight) chair: Now *that* I could ship.

☎ 02 760 20 745 ✉ Via Durini 18 🕑 10am-7pm Tue-Sat Ⓜ San Babila

DIY DESIGN

Find your own design inspiration at these new Milanese design resources:

Design Library (2, B5; ☎ 02 581 42 500; Via Savona 11; per day €10; 🕑 10am-7.30pm Mon-Fri, 10am-5pm Sat) A design buff's dream lounge, lined with new Macintosh computers, every issue of design bibles like *Domus* and *Wallpaper* back to the '80s, Phaidon design monographs, company catalogues and more.

Fashion Library (2, B5; ☎ 02 835 60 20; 🖳 www.fashionlibrary.it; Via Vigevano 35; per day €8 ; 🕑 9.30am-7.30pm Mon- Fri) So you dimly recall a stupendous Missoni number in some ancient Italian *Vogue*? Use these archives organised by company, collection, year and magazine to track it down – or just start digging, and see what you discover.

WATCH THIS SPACE

If you think Milan is architecturally unpredictable now, wait until you see what emerges from those cocoons of construction you see around town.

- **Fondazione Nicola Trussardi** (🖳 www.fondazionenicolatrussardi.com) draws crowds with provocative art installations in public spaces by international art stars, announced on their website.
- Adjacent to the Palazzo dell'Arengario, architect Italo Rota's pavilion for the **Museo di Novecento** (3, C5; Piazza Duomo) promises to resemble a giant glass science lab beaker.
- Architecture all-stars Zaha Hadid, Arata Isozaki, Daniel Libeskind and Pier Paolo Maggiora are reinventing an industrial site near the Fiera as the massive **CityLife** complex, which by 2014 will include twisting office towers, housing, parks, even canals.
- The abandoned Ansaldo industrial complex that once housed Ferrari is being transformed by British architect David Chipperfield into **Ansaldo City of Cultures** (2, A6; Via Tortona). The public complex will include the Milan's Archaeological Museum, Centre for Advanced Studies on Visual Arts and Centre of Non-European Cultures.

Da Driade (3, D2)

Frescoed rooms present the ultimate design challenge – with all those cherubs flying around, suddenly that mod houndstooth sofa seems a bit much – but Da Driade rises to the occasion in its own converted neoclassical palazzo showroom with impeccable eclecticism, unconventional materials and top international designers.
☎ 02 760 20 359
🖳 www.driade.com
✉ Via Manzoni 30
🕓 10am-7pm Tue-Fri, 3-7pm Mon
Ⓜ Montenapoleone

Flos (3, F3)

So this is what they mean by seeing things in a different light. The showroom floor here is surreal, with rice-paper lanterns that look like sea urchins, a desk lamp shaped like a chrome horn, and a floor lamp with a gold AK47 for a base that sheds a provocative light on any subject.
☎ 02 760 01 641 ✉ Corso Monforte 9 🕓 10am-7pm Tue-Fri, 3-7pm Mon
Ⓜ San Babila

Kartell (3, E1)

Plastic hasn't got this much word of mouth since *The Graduate*. Philippe Starck brought Lucite and French baroque together at last in a clear plastic Ghost Chair perfect for post-revolutionary nobility experiencing cash-flow issues, while Missoni's starburst fabrics add more instant pop to plastic chair seats than a mislaid thumbtack.
☎ 02 659 79 16 ✉ Via Carlo Porta 1 Ⓜ Turati

Moroso (3, B1)

You half expect to glimpse Van Gogh shooting pool in the corner of this vibrant green and red gallery, with its curvaceous lipstick-coloured Ron Arad arm-chairs, verdant Venus flytrap chair, and a couch spontaneously combusting into a swirling, unstable floral pattern of red, brown and turquoise.
☎ 02 720 16 336 ✉ Via Pontaccio 8/10 🕓 10am-1pm & 2.30-7.30pm
Ⓜ Lanza

Sawaya & Moroni (3, D3)

For the host with the most, butlers use a cheap second-best to Lucite stands shaped like chandeliers, with clever shelves built in to hold champagne flutes and those tiny jars of Beluga with S&M's signature silver spoons. Come to test out Zaha Hadid's Glacier Sofa, and definitely stay for the party if you're here during Fashion Week or Salone del Mobile, when those aperitif holders see brisk use.
☎ 02 87 45 49
✉ Via Manzoni 11
🕓 10am-7pm Mon-Fri
Ⓜ Montenapoleone

NOTABLE BUILDINGS & MONUMENTS

Casa Fontana Silvestri (3, F3)

Block out the Vespa traffic and shoppers hauling Dolce & Gabbana bags, and you can imagine from this classic Lombard edifice what this street must've looked like eight centuries ago. Ornamental *cotto* (baked clay) window frames attributed to Bramante grace the spare exterior, while scowling masks in the capitals above the stone door make a dramatic entrance.
✉ Corso Venezia 10
Ⓜ San Babila

Cimitero Monumentale (2, B2)

Leave it to the Milanese to take grandeur to the grave. The striking white and black entry is an 1866 Renaissance revival, raising the spirits and status of the notables interred in these sculpture-bedecked mausoleums. Even liquor magnate David Campari can hardly be bitter, with Giannino Castiglioni's impressive bronze *Il Cenacolo* for a headstone. Grab a leaflet inside the forecourt to guide you through this graveyard gallery.
☎ 02 884 65 600 € free
⏰ 8am-6pm Tue-Sun
Ⓜ Garibaldi

Nuova Fiera di Milano Rho-Pero (2, A3)

Billowing glass sails by architect Massimiliano Fuksas ingeniously cover the oil stains where the Agip refinery once stood, and float over 1.3 kilometres of reclaimed exhibition space. A $750-million marvel of engineering made with 100,000 glass pieces, this magical megastructure levitates the bar for the Salone del Mobile and other events held here – and Italian architecture, too.
☎ 02 499 71 🖥 www .fieramilanoedintorni.it
✉ Strada Statale del Sempione 28, Rho Ⓜ Rho Fiera

Palazzo della Ragione (3, C4)

Founded in 1228 to handle deals brokered and broken in this merchants' piazza, this elegant colonnaded hall of justice bears Milan's bristled boar insignia in terracotta. Empress Maria Theresa added a layer of bricks and bureaucracy with an archive of officially notarised papers, which piled up until 1961. Now the Palazzo hosts temporary exhibitions that don't mind being upstaged by their surroundings.
✉ Piazza Mercanti
⏰ open during exhibitions; times vary Ⓜ Duomo

Palazzo Reale (3, D5)

Talk about versatile: Milan's medieval Town Hall became a Visconti villa in the 13th-century, Spanish hacienda in the 16th, Empress Maria Theresa's palace in the 18th, and WWII bombing target. Now it's being remodelled to house Milan's art collections. Meanwhile, the ground floor hosts touring exhibitions ranging from Helmut Newton: Sex & Landscapes to Caravaggio.
☎ 02 86 01 85 🖥 www .comune.milano.it/palazzo reale ✉ Piazza del Duomo 12 € around €9, depending on exhibition
⏰ 9.30am-6pm Tue-Sun
Ⓜ Duomo

Stazione Centrale – a hub of activity in a city on the move (p28)

Pirelli Skyscraper (2, D2)
The upstart that broke the rules and outgrew the Madonnina atop the Duomo is widely admired for its fine bone structure: glass skin pulled tautly over a carefully calibrated, reinforced concrete base. Lead architect Gió Ponti's landmark has not only stood the test of time for 50 years, but even withstood an accidental plane crash into the building in 2002.
✉ Piazza Duca d'Aosta Ⓜ Centrale FS

Stazione Centrale (2, E2)
Some call it mighty, others call it mighty ugly, but the 1931 Central Station is certainly the most unavoidable monument in Milan. Nearly 100 million people every year pass through these hulking portals, up escalators past Fascist mosaics extolling the virtues of Lombardy (mostly culinary), and onward to train platforms and parts unknown.
✉ Piazza Duca d'Aosta Ⓜ Centrale FS

Torre Branca (2, B3)
The spindly legs on this steel tower may not inspire you to take the 10-minute lift ride 108m to the viewing platform, but not to worry: Gió Ponti's 1930s engineering feat was safety-reinforced in 2003. Go at night to watch lights twinkle, and lord it over the Just Cavalli Caffé bouncers below.
✉ Via Camoens, Parco Sempione; next to Triennale € lift ticket €3 ✆ 9.30pm-1am Tue-Sun; also 10.30am-12.30pm & 4pm-6.30pm Wed, 2.30-6pm Fri, 10.30am-2pm Sat-Sun, (2.30-7.30pm Sat-Sun mid-Apr–Oct) Ⓜ Cadorna

Torre Velasca (3, D6)
Is this top-heavy tower the headquarters of some superhero's archnemesis, a postmodern prison block or a watchtower for companies paranoid about corporate espionage? Studio BBPR's signature tower with a bigger, medieval-style block grafted on top was

finished in 1958, and almost half a century later, it's still fascinatingly sinister.
✉ Piazza Velasca Ⓜ Missori

CHURCHES

San Bernardino alle Ossa (3, E5)
Don't look now, but there are Milanese clamping onto window ledges with their teeth here as though their lives depend on it. Luckily, that's not the case: all of them were long dead when their skeletons were repurposed to make rococo crown mouldings of skulls in this exquisitely morbid 17th-century chapel, through the main church on your right.
✉ Piazza Santo Stefano 2 ✆ 10am-6pm Tue-Sun Ⓜ Duomo

San Francesco di Paola (3, D2)
Tucked in among sprawling temples to fashion in the Quadrilatero d'Oro, this little gem of a church

---

FASCIST OR MODERN?
Looking around at Milan's 1930s Fascist architecture, it's eerie to note just how mainstream modern it appears today. A couple of tweaks to the austere 1937 Assicurazioni Generali building in 2000, and ta-da, it's now the **Armani megastore** (3, D2; Via Alessandro Manzoni 31). With its huge, stark halls, the 1930s **Palazzo dell'Arengario** (3, C5; Piazza Duomo) is ideal for contemporary art installations, and proved the perfect foil for artist Martin Creed's deadpan humour in a neon sign reading, 'Everything is going to be alright.' But the 1935 **Direzione Regionale Building** (2, D3; 25 Via della Moscova) is a looming reminder that Fascist edifices were built to intimidate the masses, not accommodate them – the fortress-like walls, oversized columns, and sculptures glowering from the roof would be perfect for a horror film set, if they weren't busy housing the EU Finance Ministry. The most convincing argument against Fascist aesthetics is the **Via Giuseppe Marcova Carabinieri** (2, D3) post: a square box with a grotesquely fascinating frieze of screaming eagles, AK47s, grenades, bombs and gas masks.

Sant'Eustorgio – styles fuse to form a heavenly harmony

outshines Armani's glittering megastore across the street. Although commissioned by the Minimi order in 1728, it's hardly minimalist, but tricked out in Baroque pomp with gilt galore, a graceful 1890 neoclassical façade, and a chapel altarpiece by Guerini.

☒ Via Manzoni 3
☼ 9am-noon & 4-6.30pm
Ⓜ Montenapoleone

San Lorenzo alle Colonne (2, C5)

Like charming old gents chatting on the front steps weekdays, this place has only got better-looking since the fall of Rome. A freestanding row of 16 Corinthian columns salvaged from Milan's pagan past hints at the crumbling Roman grandeur inside, including the octagonal Cappella di Sant'Aquilino's expressive 4th-century mosaics of big-eared saints.
☒ Corso di Porta Ticinese 39 ☼ 7.30am-12.30pm & 2.30-6.45pm Ⓜ Missori

San Maurizio (2, C4)

Through a door by the altar lies Milan's hidden crown jewel: the restored 16th-century royal chapel. Bernardino Luini's breathtaking frescoes immortalise Milan's literary star, Ippolita Sforza, and her family, alongside blissful martyred women saints – note Santa Lucia calmly holding her lost eyes, and Santa Agata casually carrying her breasts on a platter.
☒ Corso Magenta 15
☼ 9am-noon & 2-5.30pm Tue-Sun Ⓜ Cadorna

Sant'Eustorgio (2, C5)

Like Milan's fusion restaurants, this façade is a mish-mash of styles that somehow works. Sant'Eustorgio was built in the 9th century, updated in the 11th, boosted with Bramante's baptistery in the 15th, and given a neo-Romanesque look in the 19th; today, its harmonious exterior belies its rabble-rousing past as Milan's Inquisition centre.
☒ Piazza Sant'Eustorgio
Ⓜ Porta Venezia

PARKS

Giardini Pubblici (2, D3)

A whole life story unfolds as you follow pebble paths past a kiddie carnival of bumper cars, bungee swings and a carousel, onward to pick-up games of footie, canoodling teens, a beer kiosk, baby prams and jogging paths. Feel free to jump in wherever you like, or just stop and smell the roses.
☼ 6.30am-sunset Ⓜ Palestro

Orto Botanico (3, C2)

The towering gingko here is the arboreal pride of Milano, surrounded by (perfectly legal) medicinal plants. An afternoon in their fragrant midst may not add years to your life, but it certainly adds to the overall quality.
☒ Via Brera 28; entry through Accademia di Brera
☼ 9am-noon & 1-4pm Mon-Fri Ⓜ Lanza

Parco delle Basiliche (2, C5)

Dodge the shoppers along Corso Porta Ticinese and take the scenic route from San Lorenzo past the Museo Diocesano to Sant'Eustorgio, past couples, clusters of gossips, and children running circles around their parents.
Ⓜ Porta Venezia

Parco Sempione (2, B3)

Everything you'd expect from Milan is here, and grass too: a historic castle (Castello Sforzesco, p19), chic bars (p65), a museum honouring design (Triennale, p23), lovely Liberty-style buildings (Acquario, p31) and an architectural conversation piece (Torre Branca, p28).

🕙 6.30am-8pm Nov-Feb, to 9pm Mar, Apr & Oct, to 10pm May, to 11.30pm Jun-Sep Ⓜ Cadorna

SPAS & WELLNESS

Aquae Calidae (2, C5)
You can't argue with the divine massages, but these ritualised Roman baths are sometimes too authentic. Instead of the usual bachelor party, this spa suggests a Roman-style steambath with 10 of your closest pals, and a 'farewell to spinsterhood' bachelorette party involving saffron tunics and nut-strewn floors. Um, is Greco-Roman wrestling allowed? Because that could get interesting.
🖳 www.aquaecalidae.it ⊠ Via Santa Sofia 14 € massage €50-80 🕙 women 2-11pm Mon &Thu, men 2-11pm Wed & Fri; both 11am-8pm Sat-Sun Ⓜ Crochetta

Bulgari E'Spa (3, C2)
The world's a stage, and you're the star – at least while you're perched on a wicker chaise longue by the emerald hammam, bathing in the glow of candles or the gold-mosaic pool, waiting to be waited on hand and foot with a four-handed massage. As long as you're a star, you won't mind the astronomical prices for brief, intense massages and soothing facials. Call to book your appointment.
☎ 02 805 80 52 00 🖳 www.bulgarihotels.com ⊠ Via Privata Fratelli Gabba 7B € facial €105, massage €105-250 Ⓜ Montenapoleone

Dolce & Gabbana Beauty Farm (3, F3)
Spas are for rookies: these days, beauty cognoscenti prefer serious grooming usually reserved for champion racehorses. Treatments such as the somewhat daunting 60-minute 'remodelling face flash' and 80-minute 'Senritsu body firming' are accomplished with the latest Kanebo products, in a clinical setting that inspires trust in technology. Spend a day on the Beauty Farm, and emerge scrubbed, massaged, manipedicured and fresh-faced.
☎ 02 760 01 348 ⊠ Corso Venezia 15 € treatments from €80, full day €280 🕙 2-7pm Mon, 10am-9pm Tue & Fri, 10am-7pm Wed, Thu & Sat Ⓜ San Babila

ESPA at Gianfranco Ferré (3, E2)
No luxury is overlooked at this beyond-fabulous spa, bedecked in gold-and-black mosaic with custom-built relaxation chairs overlooking a private garden. Chromatherapy lights turn your shower into a liquid rainbow, and subtle aromatic oils pervade the atmosphere. Take your sweet time soaking up the ambience with a Life-Saving Back Massage (€90) or

---

HAIR APPARENT

Let your hair stand out or up for itself, and you'll fit right in among fashion-forward Milanese. But first, two handy Italian expressions: *Non troppo corti, per favore* (Not too short, please) and *No cresta, grazie* (No Mohawk, thanks). Got that? Now here's where you can get tressed to impress:

Antica Barbiera Colla (3, D3; ☎ 02 87 43 12; Via G Morone 3; 🕙 8.30am-12.30pm & 2.30-7pm Tue-Sat) Legendary barbershop off Via Manzoni, with the wood-panelled, leather-upholstered decor of a gentleman's club.

Estiló (2, B5; ☎ 02 581 03 380; Via Vigevano 14; 🕙 10am-7.30pm Tue-Wed, 10am-8pm Thu-Fri, 10am-6.30pm Sat) The shag stops here for just €18, with friendly stylists and fun cuts near Navigli.

Franco (3, D2; ☎ 02 659 58 61; Via G Pisoni 2; 🕙 9.15am-7pm Tue, Wed, Fri; 9.15am-8.30pm Thu; 10am-6.30pm Sat) Where savvy fashionistas get a new Aveda hair colour and swingy cut for under €100, right in the Quadrilatero d'Oro.

Intrecci (3, D6; ☎ 02 720 22 316; Via Larga 2; 🕙 11am-9pm Mon, 11am-11pm Tue-Sat, 10am-8pm Sun) Central, cutting-edge, and open until 11pm weeknights, in case you get a post-aperitivi urge for wild hair.

the mud wrap and scalp massage (€110).
☎ 02 760 17 526 🖳 www .gianfrancoferre.com ✉ Via Sant'Andrea 15 € massage €90-110 🕑 women 10am-4.30pm Mon & Thu, 10am-10pm Tue, Wed & Fri, 10am-9pm Sat, 11am-6pm Sun; men 5.30-10pm Mon & Thu Ⓜ San Babila

Habits Culti (2, A4)
Vestal virgins and others in tension-producing jobs find release at last in this wellness sanctuary, with altar-like platform baths that suggest you might receive an oracle with your hammam treatment (€90 to €150). Couples therapy is actually productive in side-by-side baths (€110 for two), and even if mineral water massages (€80 to €130) may not 'open your mind' as promised, they'll surely win over skeptics.

☎ 02 485 17 588
✉ Via Angelo Mauri 5
€ baths per couple €110, hammam €90-150, massage €80-130 🕑 10am-10pm; no treatments Sat
Ⓜ Conciliazione

MILAN FOR CHILDREN

Kids have the run of every park and piazza in Milan: the under 12s have the grounds to themselves (as long as they're accompanied by one parent!) outside the Villa Belgiojoso Bonaparte housing the **Galleria d'Arte Moderna** (3, F1; Via Palestro 16; 🕑 7am-6pm Tue-Sun), and the teen hangout of choice is outside San Lorenzo alle Colonne, skateboard optional. If you'd like a grown-up time at the opera or spa, check the English-language *Hello*

Milano classifieds at www .hellomilano.it. Try the *English Yellow Pages* found in the foreign-language section of any Milanese bookstore (p48) to find English-speaking children's activities and playgroups, nannies and babysitters.

Civico Acquario (2, C3)
You'll be transfixed by the aquatic Art Nouveau façade, but kids will race ahead to see Lombardy's fish on display at Europe's third oldest aquarium. Turns out Lombard mountain streams and canals make for rather predictable silvery fish, but that only makes the red anemones more splashy, the archway of fish more dramatic, and the balletic boarfish become real prima donnas.

☎ 02 864 62 051 ✉ Viale Gadio 2 🕑 9.30am-6pm
Ⓜ Lanza

Bumper-to-bumper in Parco Sempione (p29)

Museo Civico di Storia Naturale (2, D3)
One word revives kids bored of shopping and sightseeing: dinosaurs! Seven of them are here at Italy's oldest museum, along with dino eggs, fossils and gems. Upstairs, old-fashioned zoology dioramas showcase lifelike taxidermied critters, along with the latest insights about conservation and endangered species.
☎ 02 884 63 280 ⊠ Corso Venezia 55 € €3/free; free after 2pm Fri ⊕ 9am-5pm Tue-Sun Ⓜ Palestro

Museo Nazionale della Scienza e della Tecnica (2, B4)
Kids of every age ooh and ahh over the latest and greatest inventions from Leonardo da Vinci to today. Downstairs are spooky medieval forges, whilst upstairs robotics and models are testing Leonardo's outlandish designs – those starched wings don't fly, but that anteater-shaped copper cooling device actually works. Out back you will find a train station full of steam engines and a 1940s submarine that you can tour, if you book ahead.
☎ 02 485 55 12 00 ⌨ www.museoscienza .org ⊠ Via San Vittore 21 € family/adult/child €8/6/3 ⊕ 9.30am-5pm Tue-Fri, 9.30am-6.30pm Sat-Sun Ⓜ Sant'Ambrogio

MILAN'S HIDDEN SPLENDOURS
'The city of art and design is also a city of secret beauty,' says Rosella Ghezzi, renowned art critic for *ViVi Milano*, the indispensable cultural supplement of *Corriere della Sera*. 'Fragmented and stratified though it is, traces of its history are woven into this urban fabric, and hidden getaways await discovery.' These are among her personal favourites:
• Bernardino Luini frescoes at San Maurizio (p29).
• Museo Bagatti Valsecchi (p21).
• Fourth-century mosaics of the Cappella di Sant'Aquilino, in San Lorenzo alle Colonne (p29).
• Secret passageways in the Castello Sforzesco (p19).
• Bramante cloister at Santa Maria delle Grazie (p13), 'and the perfume of its magnolias in April'.
• The Orto Botanico (p29), 'an unexpected oasis of green with the most ancient gingko biloba tree in Europe'.
• The furthermost stretches of the Navigli (p17).
• Galleria Milano (p24), 'modern and contemporary art in a frescoed neoclassical palace'.
• Boccascena Caffè (p62) at Palazzo Litta, with its jewelbox theatre and courtyard tables.
• Cantiere dei Sensi (p63), where the furnishings and design pieces are for sale.

Discover hidden gems along Milan's Navigli

Trips & Tours

WALKING TOURS
Head-to-Toe Milano

Get a heady start at the **Biblioteca Ambrosiana** (**1**; p18) to see Rembrandt pulling faces in his self-portraits. Make like a medieval head of state and pay a visit to the **Palazzo della Ragione** (**2**; p27) to pay your respects to the boar that started the city, then onward to Piazza della Scala to honour the city's second most famous former resident, at the **Leonardo da Vinci statue** (**3**).

An eye for fashion watches from a billboard

A fine head of hair is just around the corner for men at **Antica Barbiera Colla** (**4**; p30), where your new style is bound to be smarter than the bowl-cut of Moroso's famous *Knight in Black* just up the block at **Museo Poldi-Pezzoli** (**5**; p22). Exciting doings are afoot at **Gallo** (**6**; p45), the couture socks maker, and **Armani Jeans Caffé** (**7**; p57) is a wise choice for lunch just before your pedicure appointment around at **Franco** (**8**; p30). Head up to **Padliglione d'Arte Contemporanea** (**9**; p22), just a few blocks away and well ahead of conventional thinking, then onto **Galleria d'Arte Moderna** (**10**; p21), with its twinkly eyed neoclassical portraits and forward-thinking futurists.

Hot-foot it back to Via della Spiga for hats at **Alan Journo** (**11**; p46) and espresso at **Just Cavalli Bar** (**12**; p65), before getting a headful of fresh ideas at **Galleria Corsoveneziaotto** (**13**; p24). If you can foot the bill, pick up outrageous shoes at **Prada** (**14**; p40), or let a little bubbly go to your head at **Caffé Cova** (**15**; p57).

Distance 2.5km **duration** 4-5 hours ▶ **start** Biblioteca Ambrosiana Ⓜ Duomo ● **end** Caffé Cova Ⓜ Monte Napoleone

Visit Santa Maria delle Grazie and crack the da Vinci code

Milan, Body & Soul

A heavenly day begins with cappuccino at **Zucca in Galleria** (**1**; p57) and a pilgrimage to the magnificent **Duomo** (**2**; p10). Bramante's small wonder **Santa Maria presso San Satiro** (**3**; p15) is around the corner – and as if your jaw isn't already tired from all that dropping, turn the corner and enter **Peck** (**4**; p49), Milan's gourmet garden of earthly delights. Head next to Via Meravigli (literally 'street of miracles') and detour to **La Brisa** (**5**; p58) for a leisurely fusion lunch before you duck into **San Maurizio** (**6**; p29) to glimpse Luni's blissful martyrs – they've lost some rather key body parts, yet effortlessly rise above it all. But as long as your tongue is blessedly intact, put it to work on hot-pepper-chocolate gelato at nearby **Chocolat** (**7**; p58).

Now you're fortified for **Il Cenacolo** (**8**; p13), an evermore ethereal experience as the apostles fade to a tantalising shadow of their former selves, while a Titian Madonna leaps off the wall in living colour at **Santa Maria delle Grazie** (**9**; p13) next door. Thus uplifted, you'll float down the street to **Noy** (**10**; p61) for aperitivi and onward to **Habits Culti** (**11**; p31) for a water massage to undo today's sensory overload.

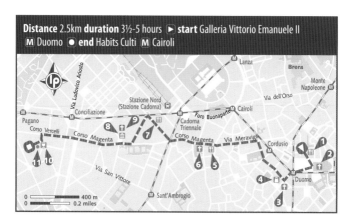

Distance 2.5km **duration** 3½-5 hours ▶ **start** Galleria Vittorio Emanuele II Ⓜ Duomo ● **end** Habits Culti Ⓜ Cairoli

Time-Travel Milan

Flashback to 1975 bell-bottoms at the **Fashion Library** (**1**; p25), then fast-forward to emerging designers **Brusaferri** (**2**; p45) and **Salvatore & Marie** (**3**; p42) for a peek into the fashion future. Leave 21st-century traffic behind and head for the Naviglio Grande, Milan's super-highway c 1500. Here you'll discover your once-and-future living room at **Mauro Bolognesi** (**4**; p47), where yellow vinyl recliners are set for a comeback.

Ancient beauty of San Lorenzo alle Colonne

Nearby is **Be Bop** (**5**; p55), where a trendy crowd devours old-world wood-fired pizza within stylish walls made from old floors. Stop at **Rivareno** (**6**; p58) for artisanal gelato made the time-honoured way, and a timely glance at your email. Afterwards, see if you can tell which of **Sant'Eustorgio's** (**7**; p29) architectural details date from the Middle Ages, Renaissance and 19th century, then check out architect Massimilano Fuksas' futuristic lipgloss-red design for **Armani Jeans Caffè** (**8**; p57) over espresso.

Stroll through the **Museo Diocesano's** (**9**; p22) serene white cloisters and collection of Renaissance paintings, then head back to the bustle of Corso di Porta Ticense and next season's collections from Milanese designers **Mauro Leoni** (**10**; p44) and **Anna Fabiano** (**11**; p42). Watch skateboarders do the latest tricks under ancient Roman columns at **San Lorenzo alle Colonne** (**12**; p29), then explore technology past, present and future at **Museo Nazionale della Scienza e della Tecnica** (**13**; p32) – and get cracking on that time machine.

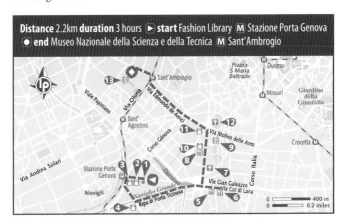

Distance 2.2km **duration** 3 hours ▶ **start** Fashion Library Ⓜ Stazione Porta Genova
● **end** Museo Nazionale della Scienza e della Tecnica Ⓜ Sant'Ambrogio

DAY TRIPS
Bellagio (4, B1)

Let's set the record straight: this **Lake Como** town was dashingly handsome long before George Clooney moved here. The gregarious peninsula reaches out to greet visitors as they drift past on boats, and it's impossible not to be smitten by Bellagio's inviting waterfront, rugged, zigzagging streets, sunbaked, red-roofed buildings, lush **cypress groves** and gardens.

'Where for art thou?', Verona (opposite)

You can get up close and personal with the entire town in an hour or two, leaving you with blessedly little to do other than enjoy a leisurely lunch, wander aimlessly, while away the afternoon at a lakeside café, or hop the slow boat back to Como. Twelfth-century **San Giacomo** has lost none of its Lombard high Romanesque charms, and you can also explore two of Bellagio's most splendid villas: **Villa Serbelloni** (☼11am & 4pm Tue-Sun in fair weather) and **Villa Melzi** (☎03 195 1281; €5; ☼9am-6.30pm end Mar-Oct) with its magnificent gardens and Egpytian art collection. Not to be too forward, but you'll probably want to stay the night here or drift over to **Varenna** where room rates are lower.

INFORMATION
75km north of Milan

- 🖳 www.bellagiolakecomo.com
- 🚆 Trains depart hourly from Milan's Stazione Centrale to Como Stazione San Giovanni station (40 minutes). From station, take hourly hydrofoil (45 minutes), bus (75 minutes), or scenic ferry (two hours) to Bellagio.
- 🚗 A8, then A9 after Lainate; at Como, take exit Sud for lakeside road S583. Travel time about 1½ hours (depending on traffic).
- ⚓ Navigazione Lago di Como (☎03 157 92 11; Piazza Cavour) operates ferries and hydrofoils year-round.
- ⓘ Tourist office (☎03 195 0204; Piazza Mazzini; ☼9am-1pm & 2.30-6pm Mon-Sat)

Bergamo (4, C2)

When Italians praise Bergamo's elusive charm, they don't just meant that arcane Bergamasco dialect. This staunchly independent split-level stronghold was its own Venetian city-state in the Alpine foothills, and when you take the **funicular** up to **Città Alta**, you'll enter a world apart. Glimpse the city's chequered Venetian past in the diamond-patterned **Cappella Colleoni**, and on your way out through the gate, tickle the testicles on the family crest for good luck – all three of them.

The **Piazza Vecchia** is a majestic medieval square and the ideal location to savour some cat's tongues – **lingue di gatti**, buttery biscotti that melt on your tongue in oddly French fashion. You're all but required by law to sample local **taleggio** cheese and **Bergamascha** wine at one of the *enotecas* (tasting rooms) along Via Colleoni before you take the next funicular up to **San Vigilio** hill for a hike, or downhill to modern **Città Bassa**. Prepare to be wowed here by the Botticelli, Fra Angelico, Raphael, Bellini and Lotto masterpieces stashed away in the **Accademia Carrara**, and see why the Galleria d'Arte Moderna has gained a reputation like Bergamo's: full of intriguing surprises.

INFORMATION
58km northeast of Milan

- 🚌 Bergamo's bus station (☎ 03 524 02 40; 🖳 www.sab-autoservizi.it; Piazzale G Marconi, SAB) operates services to the lakes and mountains and to/from Milan's Piazza Castello (€4, every half-hour).
- 🚆 Trains between Milan's Stazione Centrale and Piazzale G Marconi train station (€3.50, 45 minutes, trains almost hourly – see 🖳 www.trenitalia.it for schedule.). From station, take funicular to Cittá Alta.
- 🚗 A4 autostrada or S11, follow the *Città Alta* signs for the old city.
- ℹ️ Tourist Office (☎ 03 524 2226; 🖳 www.apt.bergamo.it; Via Gombito 13; 🕑 Mon-Fri 9am-12.30pm & 2-5.30pm)

Verona (4, F3)

Plenty of places claim to be for lovers, but Verona isn't kidding. The whole city is an architectural aphrodisiac, with fairy-tale palazzos of striped brick and marble and narrow, secretive streets. Legend has it that the real-life Romeo and Juliet lived here, and you can visit the **Casa di Giulietta**, the site of countless pledges of undying love – some of them sincere. Rediscover the thrill of the chase in the **Giardino Giusti** maze, bumping into statues of mythological beasts at every turn.

This is a city that knows how to work an emotion, even when summer opera in the Roman ampitheatre has ended. Titian's **Assumption** in the Duomo could move a stone to rapture, while Mantegna's moving altar in **San Zemo** might make it bipolar. Stand among the flower vendors in **Palazzo delle Erbe** to take in 360-degree Renaissance charm, or head to **Scaligeri Palazzo** to pay your respects to Dante, the poet who braved the inferno for love and found peace here. One more glass of Verona's courage-gathering **Amarone** wine, and you may be moved to declare from balconies your affection for fair Verona, where we lay our scene.

INFORMATION
161km east of Milan

- 🖳 http://portale.comune.verona.it
- 🚆 Dozens of trains depart daily from Milan's Stazione Centrale to Verona's Porta Nuova:(€11.50, 1 hr 35 minutes, see 🖳 www.trenitalia.it for schedule). From station, take bus 11, 12, 13, 14, 72 or 73 to centre.
- 🚗 A4 toward Venice, exit Verona Sud; follow signs to town centre.
- 🕑 9am-6pm Mon-Sat & 9am-3pm Sun
- ℹ️ Tourist office (☎ 045 806 8680; Piazza Brá or Porta Nuova; 🖳 iinfo@tourism.verona.it)

Grandiose graves at Cimitero Monumentale

ORGANISED TOURS

Accademia di Italiano

This centre offers Italian language study programmes with irresistible incentives: your next dinner, football match or outfit depends on it. Pick up the lingo as you cook classic Italian recipes, hit the soccer pitch or design a dress – bet you won't make the same mistake twice.

☎ 02 873 88 760

🖳 www.aimilano.it ✉ Via P. Paleocapa 1 € usually €400 per week/€490 for 2 weeks, plus €60 enrolment fee Ⓜ Cadorna

Select Italy

If you'd rather spend your precious vacation time in Milan with opera divas, Leonardo da Vinci and personal shoppers than tour guides droning on about dates to cranky crowds, try these offbeat walking tours with no more than eight

fellow travellers. 'Heavenly Music' introduces you to maestros and mezzo-sopranos at Milan's Casa Verdi Home, the world's first retirement centre for musicians (US$95 per person/US$370 solo); solve the Da Vinci code and deconstruct Bramante on tour with Milan's masters of invention (US$95 per person/US$370 solo); 'The Simplest of Tastes' is anything but, courtesy of a former fashion exec turned personal shopper (US$95 per person/US$541 half-day). Custom tours available.

☎ +1 847 853 1661

🖳 http://selectitaly.com

A Friend in Milan

Not much for matching blue hats and canned jokes over the tour bus intercom? Get an insider's take on Milan instead. Customise your own itinerary by foot or car with an English-speaking local and cover major monuments, bargain shopping,

maybe a haircut – but remember you'll be paying €50 per hour for the privilege of your companion's company.

☎ +44 39 348 600 6298

🖳 www.friendinmilan.co.uk

Look Mi

So you couldn't get reservations for da Vinci's *Il Cenacolo* and it's your last day in Milan? All aboard this three-hour bus tour, covering *Il Cenacolo*, La Scala and Cimitero Monumentale. Tours depart at 9.30am Tuesday to Sunday (except for the last two weeks in August) from in front of the APT tourist office on Piazza del Duomo (corner of Via Marconi). Tickets cost €50, including hotel pick-up and drop-off, guaranteed admission to *Il Cenacolo* and all monuments. Information and tickets available online, or from the APT tourist office.

☎ 02 339 10 794

🖳 www.autostradale.it

Shopping

Yes, it's every bit as good as you've heard it is and probably better. Milan's gourmet shops will have you lying to agricultural inspectors about the salami in your suitcase, and Mephisphelean Milanese designers will tempt you to defy your air carrier's weight limit with must-have home furnishings and stunning art books – not to mention all those shoes.

You don't have to be a clotheshorse to savour the thrill of spotting high fashion here in its native habitat. Window-shop the Quadrilatero d'Oro with giraffe-scale models in T-shirts and flip-flops, still in their runway make-up, or cruise Corso Porta Ticinese with skateboarding art-punks sneaking covetous glances at one another's accessories. In the independent design studios around Porta Genova, you might even discover that ever-elusive quarry: the next Prada. Sure, you can get your Gucci in London just as easily as in Milan, but you'll never see it worn so well – and you wouldn't want to miss out on the sales in January and June.

Even if you live to shop, go ahead and linger over Sunday brunch and sleep late Monday morning, since most shops are closed Sundays and don't open until Monday 3pm. In the Quadrilatero d'Oro most shops are open Monday through Saturday 10am to 7pm. Outside the Quadrilatero d'Oro, most shops are closed between noon and 3pm daily for *la pausa* (lunch and siesta).

CLOTHING & SHOE SIZES

Women's Clothing

Aust/UK	8	10	12	14	16	18
Europe	36	38	40	42	44	46
Japan	5	7	9	11	13	15
USA	6	8	10	12	14	16

Women's Shoes

Aust/USA	5	6	7	8	9	10
Europe	35	36	37	38	39	40
France	35	36	38	39	40	42
Japan	22	23	24	25	26	27
UK	3½	4½	5½	6½	7½	8½

Measurements approximate only;
try before you buy.

Men's Clothing

Aust	92	96	100	104	108	112
Europe	46	48	50	52	54	56
Japan	S	M	M		L	
UK/USA	35	36	37	38	39	40

Men's Shirts (Collar Sizes)

Aust/Japan	38	39	40	41	42	43
Europe	38	39	40	41	42	43
UK/USA	15	15½	16	16½	17	17½

Men's Shoes

Aust/UK	7	8	9	10	11	12
Europe	41	42	43	44½	46	47
Japan	26	27	27.5	28	29	30
USA	7½	8½	9½	10½	11½	12½

MONDO MODA

In case you can't find these top 20 Italian-gone-global designers back home, here's where you can find them in Milan. Except where noted, these flagship stores are open 10am to 7pm Monday to Saturday and are located in the Quadrilatero d'Oro near the San Babila and Monte Napoleone Metro stops; prices range from staggering to surprisingly reasonable.

Alberta Ferretti (3, D2; ☎ 02 760 03 095; Via Monte Napoleone 21/A Ⓜ Monte Napoleone) Clever cuts in voluptuous fabrics, for that hottie brainiac look.

Armani (3, D2; ☎ 02 723 18 600; megastore Via Manzoni 31 Ⓜ Monte Napoleone) Sleek lines and impeccable cuts.

Costume National (3, E3; ☎ 02 760 18 356; Via Sant'Andrea 12 Ⓜ San Babila) Sculpted flats, pedestal trousers and other wearable architecture.

Diesel Corso Venezia (3, F3; ☎ 02 760 06 233; Corso Venezia 7/1; Ⓜ San Babila); Corso di Porta Ticinese (2, C5; ☎ 02 894 20 916; Corso di Porta Ticinese 60; Ⓜ Porta Genova) Dark jeans for pale hipsters. Corso di Porta Ticinese branch stocks 55DSL skate/sportswear line.

Dolce & Gabbana Via della Spiga (3, F3; ☎ 02 760 01 155; Via della Spiga 26 Ⓜ San Babila); Corso Venezia (3, E2; ☎ 02 760 28 485; Corso Venezia 15; Ⓜ San Babila) Where glitz meets sex appeal. Corso Venezia branch stocks ready-to-wear D&G.

Emilio Pucci (3, E3; ☎ 02 763 18 356; Via Monte Napoleone 14; Ⓜ Monte Napoleone) Acid-trip hip from the undisputed master of psychedelic prints.

Ermenegildo Zegna (3, D3; ☎ 02 760 06 437; Via Pietro Verri 3; Ⓜ San Babila) Have you been working out, or just buying Zegna suits?

Fendi (3, F2; ☎ 02 760 21 617; Via Sant'Andrea 16; Ⓜ San Babila) Maker of the indispensable baguette handbag.

Gianfranco Ferré (3, E3; ☎ 02 78 04 06; Via Sant'Andrea 15 Ⓜ Monte Napoleone) If you've got it, flaunt it in fearless colours and extravagant details.

Gucci (3, E3; ☎ 02 77 12 71; Via Monte Napoleone 5/7; Ⓜ Monte Napoleone) Synonymous with glittering excess, in a good way.

Missoni (3, E3; ☎ 02 760 03 555; Via Sant'Andrea 2; Ⓜ Monte Napoleone) Lighter-than-air knitwear in signature zig-zags and sensational colours.

Moschino (3, E2; ☎ 02 760 00 832; Via Sant'Andrea 12 Ⓜ Monte Napoleone) Instant attitude from the maestro of fake fur and graffiti slogans.

Prada Monte Napoleone (3, E3; ☎ 02 777 17 71; Monte Napoleone 8; Ⓜ San Babila); Miu Miu ready-to-wear (3, F2; Via della Spiga 13 Ⓜ San Babila) Dress like you own a gallery in minimalist clothes and high-concept shoes.

Roberto Cavalli (3, E2; ☎ 02 760 20 900; Via della Spiga 42; Ⓜ Monte Napoleone); Just Cavalli (3, E2; ☎ 02 763 16 566; Via della Spiga 30; Ⓜ Monte Napoleone) Vamp it up in trademark animal prints and bejeweled jeans.

Valentino (3, D2; ☎ 02 760 20 285; Via Monte Napoleone 20; Ⓜ Monte Napoleone) Hollywood's best red-carpet glamour since 1960.

Versace (3, E3; ☎ 02 760 08 528; Via Monte Napoleone 11; Ⓜ Monte Napoleone) Gaudy, over-the-top, and loving every minute of it.

CLOTHING

Biffi (2, B5)
Where fashion-conscious Milanese get their unfair advantage over the rest of us: Dries Van Noten suits in industrial fabrics reinforced with metal, aerodynamically engineered Comme des Garcons wraps and the latest getups from up-and-coming designers from Italy to Brazil.
☎ 02 831 16 01
✉ Corso Génova 5 & 6
Ⓜ Sant'Ambrogio

Ethic (2, C5)
Streetsmarts meet ethnic flair halfway here, with breezy bias-cut dresses in great graphic prints and funky tiered necklaces. Wear yours someplace sultry – at these prices, you can start saving for an airfare.
☎ 02 581 05 669
✉ Porta Ticinese 50
Ⓜ Sant'Ambrogio

Frip (2, C5)
Ever wonder what Kate Moss and Johnny Depp wore when they were trashing hotel suites? This edgy '80s-style store gives some idea: green satin dresses with unfinished hems worn alone or over Acme Action Jeans; PVC tuxedo collars atop torn T-shirts with 'This isn't a f***ing Gucci T-shirt' slogans.
☎ 02 832 13 60 ✉ Corso di Porta Ticinese 16 Ⓜ Missori

Love Therapy (3, E4)
Back in the '80s, designer Elio Fiorucci was all about cherub T-shirts and red jeans – but now he has moved on to garden gnomes

Fashionistas flock to 10 Corso Como (p46)

and gotten into Love Therapy. You will too, with gnome T-shirts for adults and children, funky Irregular Choice metallic flats, and orange and green Orla Kiely raincoats for strutting stylishly in storms.
☎ 02 760 91 237 ✉ Corso Europa at Piazza San Babila Ⓜ San Babila

Luisa Beccaria (3, B1)
If ever you're stumped about what to wear to a wedding, here's your answer. Make an Audrey Hepburn entrance in diaphanous silk that floats right off the shoulders, custom-designed for shameless figure flattery.
☎ 02 86 38 07 ▯ www .luisabeccaria.it ✉ Via Fiori Chiari 17 Ⓜ Lanza

Patrizia Pepe (3, E2)
Who can be bothered with all those flounces and bows on the metro? Patrizia Pepe gets what urban women

really want – feminine tailoring – and makes it snappy. Her cuts are curvy and colours clever, with a certain refinement that shows who's in control here, and she's perfectly capable of pulling off cream leather knickerbockers.
☎ 02 760 14 477 ▯ www .patriziapepe.it ✉ Via Manzoni 38 Ⓜ Monte Napoleone

Pietro Brunelli Maternity Appeal (3, B1)
Bump movie stars right off the best-dressed list with body-skimming designs that showcase your latest creative endeavour. The aqua silk dress with tiny pleats right below the bustline would make JLo jealous, and the belly-baring olive green halter could upstage Angelina.
☎ 02 805 42 95 ▯ www .pietrobrunelli.com ✉ Via Fiori Chiari 5 Ⓜ Lanza

Gossamer knitwear at Missoni (p40)

Emerging Designers

Salvatore & Marie (2, B5)
The fashion must-haves of the future have already arrived here: outer-space orange Lucite collars, bronzed porcelain candelabra recently evolved from primordial ooze, and tank tops with detachable soft-sculpture cats that would be right at home on Tim Burton.
☎ 02 894 22 152 ⊠ Via Vigevano 33 Ⓜ Porta Genova

Trace (2, A5)
Ingenious indie designers turn old school into new cool here: yellow and brown silkscreened stripes make you stare longer than is decent at sheer, pleated white cotton schoolgirl skirts, a newfangled traditional Japanese jacket comes with an ingenious built-in ruched belt and diagonal pleats add a contrarian twist to a skirt made of regimental tie fabric.
☎ 02 896 92 721 🖳 www .tracesurface.com ⊠ Via Savona 19 Ⓜ Porta Genova

Dragoncella (2, B5)
Flattering and flirty looks with a cutting edge make Dragoncella look like Betsey Johnson's Italian love child. Unexpected details make each piece unique, such as a circle of plain white on the side of a psychedelic print dress, or red ribbon trim on a brown denim skirt hem. Unexpected prices too: almost everything is under €100.
☎ 02 581 08 715 🖳 www .dragoncella.it ⊠ Corso Cristoforo Colombo 8 Ⓜ Porta Genova

Anna Fabiano (2, C5)
Hardworking Milanese fashionistas treat themselves to these curvaceous red jackets, swingy black-and-white knit silk skirts and kicky minidresses, each under €100. 'They're lovely because they're made with love', says Anna from behind the counter, and she means it.
☎ 02 583 06 111 ⊠ Corso di Porta Ticinese 40 Ⓜ Sant'Ambrogio

Isola Show Room (2, C2)
Everything you'll see here is handmade, streetsmart and way too cool for any design school: mod enamel jewellery, limited-edition T-shirts with 'Spaghetti Club' slogans and wild-style graffiti paintings, all at starving-artist prices. Best of all are mother-daughter team Lavgon's one-of-a-kind quilted skirts with raw silk edges, and deconstructed woollen jackets – check out the vintage fabric inside the sleeves.
☎ 02 873 90 245 🖳 www .isoladellamoda.info ⊠ Via Carmagnola 7 Ⓜ Garibaldi

Martino Midali (2, C5)
Midali has a flair for delicate nips and tucks that would make any plastic surgeon jealous. His ingeniously ruched purple silk skirt nips in to make any waistline look tiny, and pin-tucking turns a plain white cotton shirt into a wonder with hundreds of tiny folds of fabric.
☎ 02 894 06 830 ⊠ Corso Porta Ticinese 87 Ⓜ Sant'Ambrogio

CATWALK CALENDAR

Time-travel is possible four times a year in Milan, when designers parade next year's fashions at Milan Fashion Week. As you might have guessed just looking around, in Milan men are well ahead of the fashion curve: the following year's fall/winter collections debut in January, and spring/summer shows are in June. Women's fall/winter collections follow in February, and women's spring/summer shows are usually in September. For event listings and individual designer showcases, check the National Chamber of Italian Fashion's website at 🖳 www.cameramoda.it/eng.

SHOES & BAGS

Hogan (3, D2)
The saving grace of cobble-stone-pounding, style-conscious Milanese, Hogan built a global reputation on fancy sneakers that are a dream to wear. Now that flair for casual finery is also found in retro peep-toe platforms and funky orange, brown and green striped bags in buttery leather. Prices are competitive with other Golden Quad designers, around €200.
☎ 02 760 11 174 ✉ Monte Napoleone 39 Ⓜ Monte Napoleone

Berluti (3, D3)
Discover a custom-made shoe for every man's passing whim: go Zen in profound seaweed-green leather, rock out in deep purple, or warm up in sun-bronzed ochre that is the essence of Italy. There is the occasional misstep, like wing-tips covered with Da Vinci code scribblings – but the streamlined, single-eyelet numbers do not miss a beat. Prices have more than adjusted for inflation since Berluti was founded way-back in 1895.

Step out in style down Corso di Porta Ticinese

☎ 02 760 28 554 ✉ Via Pietro Verri 5 Ⓜ Monte Napoleone

Furla (3, E4)
Sleek, durable leather and sleek, durable designs make Furla handbag fetishes very easy to rationalise – especially when the prices start at under €100. Recent objects of desire found here include large ultra-contemporary chocolate or vanilla tote bags bearing round buckle closures for €185, and a timeless silver clutch purse covered in a stylish embossed Islamic star pattern for €85.
☎ 02 79 69 43 ✉ Corso Vittorio Emanuele, at Via San Paolo Ⓜ Duomo

MH Way (3, F5)
Art and design acolytes worldwide adore this Japanese Italian bag designer for ingeniously compact shapes, sensational colours, technology-enhanced durability and prices that love you back. The two-storey showroom at Via Durini 2 also functions as a factory outlet, so you can snap up sample sale items for a song.
☎ 02 760 21 787 ✉ Via Durini 2 & 5 Ⓜ San Babila

Mandarina Duck (3, F4)
Nice try, Tumi and Samsonite: Mandarina Duck still does the streamlined look best, in space-age fabrics, offbeat colours, and striking shapes with rounded edges. Instead

FASHION OVERDRIVE

All you fast and furious drivers out there (you know who you are): you too can dress the part. **Tod's** (3, F2; ☎ 02 760 02 423; Via della Spiga 22; Ⓜ Monte Napoleone) is the home of the original driving shoe, in snug leather with rubber traction bumps all along the heel. Pull on your orange rubberized helmet and reinforced leather gloves from **Momo Design** (3, F4; ☎ 02 760 16 168; Galleria San Babila 4A; Ⓜ San Babila), and you're ready to take on the world in your Vespa – and if you're very bold, maybe even Milan traffic. At these prices, the €1400 Ferrari baby carriage and €780 red logo briefcase at Milan's official **Ferrari Store** (3, D4; ☎ 05 36 241044; Piazza Liberty 8; open daily 10am-8pm; Ⓜ San Babila) should come with their own pit crew. But admit it: you wish you had that €68 mini Formula One racing jacket and €195 Ferrari rocking horse when you were a kid.

of perching atop pedestals, these bags are displayed slung across furniture, just like back home – only there's probably no scrounging for change in these designer sofas.
☎ 02 78 22 10 ⊠ Galleria San Carlo, off Corso Europa Ⓜ San Babila

Mauro Leoni (2, C5)
You knew there had to be a fun, original, wearable, inexpensive shoe maker in Milan, and Mauro's it. Metallic ballet slippers with an X marking the spot across the toe, 1940s pink wing-tip pumps, red polka-dotted grosgrain heels, and orange T-strap flats,

all for less than €75…it's enough to make you forget all about that mean old Manolo and standoffish Jimmy Choo, and finally fall in love again.
⊠ Corso di Porta Ticinese 60 ◔ 3pm-7pm Mon, 10am-7.30pm Tue-Sat, 2.30pm-7.30pm Sun Ⓜ Sant'Ambrogio

La Vetrina di Beryl (2, C3)
This is what it must be like to raid the photo-shoot shoe racks at Italian *Vogue*. At just €80, Ordinary People house brand ballerina silk espadrilles keep pace with the best, including Georgina Goodman's seafoam green

crackled leather pumps with a lip like a frog's (€485) and Marc Jacobs metallic T-straps (€250).
☎ 02 65 42 78 ⊠ Via Statuto 4 Ⓜ Moscova

Le Solferine (3, C1)
Turn the sidewalk into your own personal runway in Solferine's standout shoes. Any week is Fashion Week in handcrafted boots with inlaid rhinestone heels, and it only takes two of those gold leather peep toe heels to tango.
☎ 02 655 53 52 🖳 www .lesolferine.com ⊠ Via Solferino 2 Ⓜ Lanza

OUTLET SHOPPING

No outlets in Milan? Please – that's just what other bargain-hunters say to throw you off the scent. They're not always easy to find, but strolling through Milan sure beats battling highway traffic to Fox Town outlet mall in Switzerland (though if you insist, directions are at 🖳 www.foxtown.ch).
Here's a sampling of Milan's best outlets:

Basement (3, F2; ☎ 02 763 17 913; Via Senato Damiano 15; Ⓜ Monte Napoleone) Pity the fools who paid retail for your still-stylish yellow Fendi baguette and Vivienne Westwood wrap skirt – at four times the price.

10 Corso Como Outlet (☎ 02 290 02 674; Via Tazzoli 3, through courtyard; Ⓜ Garibaldi) Last season's avant-garde fashions are still light years ahead of the curve, and 30% off.

Emporio 31 (2, A6; ☎ 02 422 25 77; 🖳 www.emporio31.com; Via Tortona 31, inside left courtyard; 10am-7pm Tue-Sun; Ⓜ Porta Genova) Milan's first outlet for designer furnishings features half-price Flos desk lamps, Bugatti espresso makers, and ViceVersa crocodile salad tossers.

EtrOutlet (2, E5; ☎ 02 550 20 218; Via Spartaco 3; Ⓜ Porta Romana) Lavish ties, cashmere tees, embellished purses and bolts of luxe fabric, all at plebeian prices.

Il Salvagente (2, E4; ☎ 02 761 10 328; Via Fratelli Bronzetti 16; Ⓜ San Babila) Instead of discounting their brands, Milan's flagship stores send their stuff straight here – hence the Prada, D&G, Versace, Ferretti and Armani. Cash only, but a little goes a long way.

Puma (2, E5; ☎ 02 599 02 227; Viale Monte Nero 22; Ⓜ Porta Romana) Sporty style for 40% less, including Philippe Starck flip-flops and limited edition Ferrari sports bags.

Vestistock (2, E3; ☎ 02 295 14 497; Via Ramazzini 11; Ⓜ Porta Venezia) All the big Italian brands plus Custo, Burberry, G-Star and YSL, at 50% to 80% off retail. Further temptation: it's open seven days.

JEWELLERY & ACCESSORIES

Anthias (2, D2)
You know that tropical wood and silver choker you loved at MoMA's gift shop, and those bronze sea anemone earrings you adored in Shibuya? Made right here at the Milan atelier of Monica Castiglioni (daughter of design maestro Achille Castiglione) and Natsuko Toyofuku. Snap up the latest styles before Tokyo and New York fashionistas – and at better prices too.
☎ 02 670 0203 🖳 www .anthiasnyc.com ✉ Via G Fara 33 Ⓜ Stazione Centrale

Brusaferri (2, B5)
Shapes so harmoniously organic, you'll almost believe deep sea-green tourmalines naturally burst from silver pods. Matteo makes each piece by hand, including black diamond earring cascades that spill onto shoulders, and holey silver rings that stack into moon-rock formations. Custom-made baubles you won't find at Bulgari, at a teensy fraction of the price.
☎ 02 4549 7114 🖳 www .brusaferri.it ✉ Via Vigevano 33 Ⓜ Porta Genova

Carmen Veca (2, C5)
Unexpected twists to be expected at Carmen Veca's atelier. Watch as she artfully coils cord around vintage octagonal black-and-white beads to make a striking choker, or strings crystal into geometric chandelier earrings. Better yet: choose your colours, beads, style, and have a signature piece made to order. The kicker? Most

pieces cost under €50.
☎ 02 581 05 363 ✉ Via Savona 1 🕒 10.30am-2pm & 4-7.30pm Ⓜ Porta Genova

Gallo (3, D2)
Even in seen-it-all Milan, a glimpse of ankle can still cause a sensation. Gallo's hot pink and orange striped knee-socks add an electric shock of colour to otherwise drab business attire, and the interlocking brown, green, and orange cube ones make your ankles look like they escaped from an Escher drawing. You'll never risk losing these limited-edition beauties in the dryer – especially at €12-35 a pop.
☎ 02 78 36 02 ✉ Via Manzoni 16 Ⓜ Monte Napoleone

Piumelli Guanti (3, C3)
These gloves come in the softest Nappa leather imaginable and every conceivable colour, and some inconceivable ones besides. The silk-lined chocolate gloves with contrasting lavender piping

Earthy costume jewellery on Via Manzoni

and tiny buttons will make you want to stand up and applaud, if only to admire your Piumelli-clad hands.
☎ 02 869 23 18 ✉ Galleria Vittorio Emanuele II Ⓜ Duomo

Telerie Roberto (2, C2)
The striped Jaipur silk scarves are a stylish steal at under €20, but the ruched, pleated, quilted local Como silk stoles (€50 plus) tempt with irresistible sheen and extreme thread count – Roberto will proudly whip out a magnifying glass to show you. This is the stuff of couture dreams, and Milan's finest curtains too.
☎ 02 659 94 20 ✉ Corso Como 3 Ⓜ Garibaldi

La Perla (3, D2)
Naughty but nice La Perla lingerie is branching out from its signature lacy bras to bathing suits that seem to be made entirely of straps.
☎ 02 760 00 460 ✉ Via Monte Napoleone 1 Ⓜ S Babila

La Perla Uomo (3, D2)
La Perla Uomo stocks high-cut silk knit boxer briefs that let men show more leg than AC Milan in motion.
☎ 02 805 30 92 ✉ Via Manzoni 17 Ⓜ Monte Napoleone

Perfumes & Beauty
Acqua di Parma (3, E2)
Better living through chemistry, with fresh scents that have worked their charms since the 1930s. The classic signature scent for men and women exudes confidence in interviews and first dates, while the unisex Amalfi Fig and Arancia di Capri are much-needed getaways for the senses.
☎ 02 760 23 307 ✉ Via Gesù 3 Ⓜ Monte Napoleone

Habits Culti (2, A4)
Stuffy offices beg to be misted with Culti's green-tea room spray, and spice-spiked candles turn ordinary bathrooms into beauty temples. Habits Culti has won a cult following for its savoury foodie scents and unapologetic florals, plus flower bouquets gone dramatic with reeds and driftwood elements.
☎ 02 485 17 588 ✉ Via Angelo Mauri 5 Ⓜ Conciliazione

Limoni(3, E4)
Binge on beauty with two floors of the most sought-after perfumes and products. Italian favourites include Perlier bath foam in yummy honey, and Pupa make-up for its winsome packaging: yank the tail of that giraffe or lion compact, and out slide trays of lip gloss and eye shadow.

HAT TRICK
The word 'millinery' is derived from Milan, where the reputation for the finest bonnets and men's straw hats dates back to the 16th century. The city's winning headgear streak continues today with **Borsalino** (3, F3; ☎ 02 760 17 072; Corso Venezia 21), which creates film-noir mystery with shady Panamas and the classic *coppola* (forward-tilting brimmed cap) glimpsed in many a Coppola film, and **Alan Journo** (3, E2; ☎ 02 760 01 309; Via della Spiga 36), who channels Fellini with lavender straw hats shaped like ziggurats.

☎ 02 78 37 85 ✉ Galleria del Corso 4, off Vittorio Emanuele II Ⓜ Duomo

DESIGN & HOMEWARES

10 Corso Como (2, C2)
Find all the gifts you wanted for your birthday: porcelain TV dinner trays, art books and a Paco Rabane dress made of blue plastic tiles (only €2371). Don't miss the, erm, objects of desire out the back – no, that's not an orange rubber caterpillar, and yes, batteries are included for €45.
☎ 02 290 02 674 💻 www.10corsocomo .com ✉ 10 Corso Como Ⓜ Garibaldi

Alessi (3, E3)
Once upon a time, household gadgets were no fun. But then Alessi started hiring daring designers like Michael Graves, Aldo Rossi and Robert Venturi in the 1980s, and now we have tea kettles that chirp like birds, red peppers that chop garlic, giant noses that hold pencils, and schoolgirls that open bottles of wine.
☎ 02 79 57 26 ✉ Corso Matteotti 9 Ⓜ San Babila

Arform (2, D3)
One-stop-shopping for that effortlessly cosmopolitan Milanese look, with superb design pieces in natural materials from Finland to Japan, New York to Milan. Pack your Marimekko flower-print napkins and your train-station GB Milan clock in your Qurz wood-panelled briefcase, and you've got fusion style in the bag.
☎ 02 655 46 91 ✉ Via Moscova 22 Ⓜ Moscova

Daal Gallery (2, F1)
Less is more in this careful selection of mod ceramics and mid-century furnishings, including a chandelier apparently fashioned from orange and white glass trumpets. Mix in occasional artworks by local artists and the look is complete.
✉ Via Conte Rosso 20, Lambrate Ⓜ Lambrate

DB Living (2, D2)
Two floors of inexpensive, whimsical design objects, including rubber radios that look bounceable and lamps made entirely of Italian comics. Introduce fun to the office with a turquoise leather case for papers, or a

pop-up plastic puzzle that doubles as a CD/DVD rack.
☎ 02 365 04189 ☐ www.dbliving.com ✉ Via Vittor Pisani 6 Ⓜ Repubblica

Lo Spazio Rossana Orlandi (2, A4)

Is it an art gallery, a design showroom, or a style boutique? Trick question – all you'll care about is getting that fantastic salvaged-wood bed frame and hand-carved hatstand home. Don't miss December's 'Tabula Rara' show of conceptual tableware by 20 international designers.
☎ 02 480 11 774 ✉ Via Matteo Bandello 14 Ⓜ Sant'Ambrogio

Mauro Bolognesi (2, B6)

It's the revival of the fittest at this vintage modern boutique. Bring back the classic bachelor pad with vintage starburst-patterned curtains and chrome lamps, or turn your den into a '60s record company waiting room with white enamel chairs with black vinyl seats and dramatic white-on-white vases.
☎ 02 837 60 28 ✉ Ripa di Porta Ticinese 47 Ⓜ Porta Genova

Moroni Gomma (3, E4)

Every plastic gizmo imaginable, and then some: credit cards that grate garlic, Kartell orange Lucite end tables, melamine bowls lined with photographic serving suggestions of popcorn or pistachios. Don't miss the 'nice price' bargains on the mezzanine.
☎ 02 79 62 20 ✉ Corso Matteotti 14 Ⓜ San Babila

Muji (2, E3)

With no logos, brown cardboard notebooks and accessories, industrial canvas jackets and backpacks, and few items over €50, Muji might make you wonder if you're still in Milan. The dead giveaway is the award-winning minimalist design, matched with Japanese flair for utilitarian materials.
☎ 02 742 81 169 ✉ Corso Buenos Aires 36 Ⓜ Porta Venezia

Nava (3, F4)

Museum stores and swanky stationers have peddled Nava designs since 1970, but now the Milan-based designer has its own showroom featuring high-style office supplies and leather goods at mass-market prices. Great pocket notebooks in glossy DayGlo colours, moulded aluminium desk sets and satchels good to go from office to art gallery openings.
☎ 02 79 45 99 ☐ www.navadesign.com ✉ Via Durini 23 Ⓜ San Babila

Specialities

Bau Per Miao (2, C3)

Bow-wow the pets back home with designer dog houses, stylish pet carriers, and sculptural scratching posts. Give some glam to your favourite furball with rhinestone-studded patent-leather collars in every colour – too bad they don't come in people sizes.
☎ 02 659 76 43 ✉ Via Solferino 25 Ⓜ Moscova

Fabriano (3, E3)

This elegant store has been making handmade paper since 1872, along with cool high quality leather-bound diaries, notepads, address books, calendars, business card holders and mouse pads.
☎ 02 763 18 754 ✉ Via Bigli 3 Ⓜ San Babila

Top-to-toe stylish *ragazzi* at I Pinco Pallino (p50)

BOOKS & MUSIC

L'Isola del Fumetto (2, C2)
In Italy, *fumetti* (comics) aren't just kids' stuff: grown men have been known to weep to discover these rare Italian comic books and hard-to-find action figures, and bargain-priced Italian translations of *Flash Gordon* and *Gli Incredibili* (*The Incredibles*) practically beg to be turned into laminated earrings and decoupage tables.
☎ 34 912 4148 ✉ Via Jacopo dal Verme 14
Ⓜ Garibaldi

Messaggerie Musicali (3, E4)
A feast for media omnivores, from CDs and DVDs in the basement (including special selections of Italian movies and singers) through English-language novels and travel on the second floor. Top off your media meal with a design mag and an espresso in the café.
☎ 02 760 55 404 ✉ Galleria del Corso 2, Corso Vittorio Emanuele II Ⓜ Duomo

Rizzoli (3, C4)
The renowned art book publisher also offers Italian literature and history in translation, plus great foreign newspapers and magazines.
☎ 02 864 61071 ✉ Galleria Vittorio Emanuele II
Ⓜ Duomo

Hoepli (3, D4)
Hanging out in Italy's largest bookstore almost gives you smarts by osmosis, with six floors and some 500,000 cookbooks, art books, science tomes, kids books and rare antiquarian books to absorb.
☎ 02 86 48 71 🖳 www .hoepli.it ✉ Via Hoepli 5
Ⓜ Duomo

MILAN BY THE BOOK

Talk about a bookish beauty: stylish Milan is also famed within Italy for its intellect. Here's a prime sampling of the books the city has inspired:

- *Accidental Death of an Anarchist* by Dario Fo – A sly, subversive comedy about what happens when a political prisoner is found dead at police headquarters, by the winner of the 1997 Nobel Prize for Literature, 2006 candidate for the Mayor of Milan and the city's unofficial court jester.
- *A Convent Tale: A Century of Sisterhood in Spanish Milan* by P Renée Baernstein – And you thought your office politics were tricky – check out the dramas that went on behind nunnery walls in Renaissance Milan.
- *Duca and the Milan Murders* by Giorgio Scerbanenco – Fans of hard-boiled crime fiction suss out Milan's dirty little secrets with one of Italy's foremost authors of *gialli*, or mysteries.
- *Foucault's Pendulum* by Umberto Eco – Eco's elaborate conspiracy unravels in Milan, involving Templars, Rosicrucians, Freemasons, and Jesuits – think of it as *The da Vinci Code* with a PhD.
- *The House of Gucci* by Sara G Forden – The stranger-than-fiction account of how the makers of luxury luggage got mixed up with mafia and murder, and then rebuilt the brand with upstart Tom Ford.
- *Leonardo da Vinci* by Sherwin B Nuland – This Penguin Lives book recounts the achievements, inventions, and obsessions of the genius.
- *Milan Since the Miracle* by John Foot – The fascinating story of Milan's comeback after WWII, and its unlikely transformation from humble auto-parts manufacturer to taste-maker capital.
- *Promessi Sposi (The Betrothed)* by Alessandro Manzoni – 1827 Italy's first modern novel is the story of two lovers and a country yearning to be united.
- *A Vittorini Omnibus* by Elio Vittorini – Stories from the Sicilian-born, adopted Milanese writer who was tossed out of the Fascist party, got jailed as a leftist, edited Italo Calvino and inspired Ernest Hemingway (who wrote the introduction).

Art Book Milano (2, F1)
Look no further for creative inspiration, including Federico Motta's mini books of minimalist spaces, compilations of German sound art, books on hospital design and a staggering selection of arty magazines. If you don't quite have time to follow your bookish bliss to Lambrate, check out Art Book in the Triennale.
☎ 02 215 97 624 🖥 www .artbookmilano.it ✉ Via Ventura 5 Ⓜ Lambrate

Buscemi Dischi (2, B4)
You can find Madonna anywhere, but how many other places stock her entire catalogue right alongside Musical Conversations from Iran and Felicia Weathers singing Verdi and Puccini arias? Tickets for local concerts by Italian and international acts are on sale here too.
☎ 02 80 41 03 🖥 www .buscemi.com ✉ Corso Magenta 31 Ⓜ Cadorna Triennale

FOOD & DRINK

Fratelli Freni (3, C5)
Did you leave your dentures in the front window of Fratelli Freni? Because that's where we found them – redone entirely in marzipan. Pick up surreal sweets shaped like figs or cacti and salami sandwiches for gifts, and grab an espresso and cannoli for yourself.
✉ Via Torino 1 Ⓜ Duomo

Pasticceria Giovanni Galli (3, B5)
Apparently, heaven can be purchased at a price of six for €4.50. *Alchechengi* are Lombardy's special cherry

tomatoes dunked in maraschino liquor and pure dark chocolate – if this won't win you over to vegetables, nothing will. Since 1880, Milanese have salivated over the *marrone* (candied chestnuts) in Galli's wooden display cases, but try the new-fangled hot-pepper chocolates too.
☎ 02 864 64 833 🖥 www .giovannigalli.com ✉ Via Victor Hugo 2 Ⓜ Duomo

Enoteca Cotti (2, C3)
This store is the Biblioteca Ambrosiana of Italian wines and spirits, with thousands of bottles in floor-to-ceiling bookcases. You'll pay for the privilege of checking out the rarer vintages, but many of them you won't find elsewhere, and you can try superb wines by the glass with a light bite in a side tasting room.
☎ 02 290 01 096 ✉ Via Solferino 42 Ⓜ Moscova

Garbagnati (3, C5)
Every day's a gourmet holiday with Garbagnati's panettone, the Milanese

Christmas speciality with the ideal ratio of savoury to sweet, fluffy bread to caramelised raisins. Make the most of a sunny day with picnic-perfect breads and pastries, or toast the good life with wine by the glass and house-made pasta.
☎ 02 864 60 672 ✉ Victor Hugo 3 Ⓜ Duomo

Peck (3, C5)
Fans of cold cuts will gape in awe at Peck's prosciutto-lined walls, and dessert devotees will pay their respects to the altar-sized sweets counter, but it would be a sin to neglect Peck's famous wine cellar, homemade ravioli and 3000 kinds of *parmigiano reggiano* (parmesan cheese).
☎ 02 802 31 61 ✉ Via Spadari 9 Ⓜ Duomo

Pralines Leonida (2, C3)
Skip the sweet talk and head directly to this artisanal chocolatier, where €10 gets you a golden gift box of spicy pepperoncino chocolate, or super-smooth Belgian chocolate with

Chocoholics and foodies unite at Peck

nutty, chewy centres. But fair warning: Leonida closes from July to September each year to travel and find inspirations for new delights.

☎ 02 454 83 302 ✉ Via Moscova 27 Ⓜ Moscova

Salumeria Zanelotti (2, B6)

Try this craving-inducing salami, and you'll see what really brings Milanese home from vacation. Using complicated contraptions of wood, iron and steel that surely belong in a museum, this authentic Navigli *salumeria* (salami-maker's shop) turns fine cuts of cured meat into their signature flower-shaped Milanese, plump, smoky links, and zesty *soppressata* (spicy salami). Apparently, lunch meat can be a revelation.

✉ Via Magolfa15 Ⓜ Porta Genova

FOR CHILDREN

Citta del Sole (3, B4)

Kids tearing through this toy store don't seem to realise their crafty parents are sneaking schooling into holidays. Inspire your little Leonardo with that puzzle and kids' book on bridges designed by da Vinci (€23); give those Bauhaus blocks (€82) to your niece and she might just become the next Zaha Hadid.

☎ 02 864 61 683 ✉ Via Orefici 13 Ⓜ Cordusio

I Pinco Pallino (3, E2)

That chandelier of glass animals must cast a powerful spell because enchanted parents surrender entire pay cheques here on hand-sewn floating silk dresses, ideal for tea parties in Wonderland, and embroidered overalls

that make any tiny terror look like Little Boy Blue. Seasoned baby shower attendees agree: Pinco Pallino's baby gear branch on Borgospesso is the next-best baby gift to three wishes.

☎ 02 78 19 31 ✉ Via della Spiga 42 & Via Borgospesso 25 Ⓜ Monte Napoleone

Il Mondo é Piccolo (2, B5)

These imaginative, well-crafted toys are just the ticket to jumpstart young minds and second childhoods. Attempting to balance the tricky Repo Man between two poles brings a new appreciation of physics principles, and wooden Hula Hoops beat gym memberships any day. Besides, it's never too late to enjoy a wheeled wooden duck on a stick.

☎ 02 581 06 086 ✉ Via Cesare da Sesto 19 Ⓜ Sant'Agostino

TO MARKET, TO MARKET

For the best buys in Milan, hit the streets. Here's where to find what when:

Fiera di Sinigalia (2, B5; Viale d'Annunzio; Ⓜ Porta Genova) The usual inexpensive imported goods, plus DJ mix CDs, vintage clothes, and funky handmade clothes and accessories by local artisans. Held 10am to 5pm Saturdays.

Mercato dell'Antiquariato di Brera (3, B1; Via Fiori Chiari; Ⓜ Lanza) Neither big nor a bargain, but a lovely place to browse for antiques in Brera. Held on the third Saturday of every month.

Mercato di Papiniano (2, A5; Viale Papiniano; Ⓜ Sant'Agostino) Food plus bargain-basement clothing and homewares; not always the best quality, but the biggest selection. Held on Tuesday mornings and Saturday mornings.

Mercato Fauché (2, A2; Via Fauché; 🚊 14) Hands down, the best deals on designer fashion in Milan, including major brand-name shoes from last season with prices moved a whole decimal point down, next season's samples, and bargain cashmere sweaters. Held Tuesday mornings and Saturdays until 5pm.

Mercatone dell'Antiquario del Naviglio Grande (2, B6; Naviglio Grande; Ⓜ Porta Genova) The biggest, best antiques market in Milan draws 400 dealers and avid collectors from across Northern Italy. Held on the last Sunday of every month.

Mercato Piazzale Lagosta (2, C1; Piazzale Lagosta; Ⓜ Zara) Isola's fun, cheap, independent-minded market features food, arts and crafts with a lively local crowd. Held on Saturday mornings.

Eating

Living proof that stylish people actually do enjoy their food is everywhere in Milan. You don't have to dine on Lombard saffron risotto and *cotoletta alla Milanese* (Milanese cutlet) to fit in either: Milanese are loyal to their taste buds, rather than their territory. Since the city has been Celtic, Roman, German, French, Spanish and Austrian in its history, outside influences are quintessentially Milanese – so

if you've come here on a culinary authenticity trip, don't miss the fusion dishes mixing Italian regional cuisine, international influences, and that unmistakable Milanese flair. You're not obliged to sample more than one course, but most locals wash down a good dinner with coffee or a digestive such as grappa or *amaro* (bitters). Cigarettes are about the only thing you won't find on the menu, thanks to strict new smoking bans. Cafés open from 7.30am until 8pm or later, while restaurants open for lunch from noon to 3pm and dinner is usually from 7pm until midnight. As they say in Milan, '*buon appetito*' and '*cin cin*' – here's to your health.

Espresso to go in the Ticinese quarter

CENTRE

Artidoro (3, A3)
Love, Italian Style €€
Strange but true: salami is an aphrodisiac at Artidoro, where platters of the local Milanese speciality with sides of *grana padano* cheese start couples cooing in the candlelight. What happens after the juicy *cotoletta alla Milanese* and flirty Lombard reds by the glass is your own business.

☎ 02 805 73 86 ☐ www .artidoro.it (in Italian) ✉ Via M Camperio 15 ☽ Mon-Sat Ⓜ Cairoli

Cracco-Peck (3, B4)
Leading-edge Lombard €€€€
It's only a matter of time until Milan names a street after chef Carlo Cracco, the master of Milanese invention. Dignitaries arriving with much fanfare in chauffeured Mercedes are quickly reduced to hushed awe

as the seasonal menu materialises: seafood pasta with espresso sauce, salt-crusted sole and dark chocolate crochettes with caviar.
☎ 02 87 67 74 ☐ www .peck.it ✉ Via Victor Hugo 4 ☽ closed lunch Sun, closed Sat & Aug Ⓜ Duomo

Don Carlos (3, D2)
Emotional Italian €€€€
Foodies get emotional about Don Carlos and not just

because many head straight here from the opera. Chef Angelo Gangemi surprises even the most jaded palate in this old-world setting, with brand-new creations like tangy eel with lemons and sultanas and reinvented classics like zesty pea soup with mint.

☎ 02 723 14 640 🖳 www
.dolcestilnovo.com ✉ Via
Alessandro Manzoni 29
☀ open for dinner only,
closed Aug Ⓜ Duomo

Emporio Armani Caffé (3, D2)

Fresco al Fresco €€
Ne cotton ne crudo (neither cooked nor raw) is the latest Milanese trend and naturally Armani is leading the charge with organic seasonal vegetables, fresh seafood and seared grass-fed beef served by male-model waiters. Join fashionistas kerbside with miniature schnauzers licking their faces – yes, the octopus, green bean and lemon salad is that good.

☎ 02 723 18 680 ✉ Via
Crocerossa 2 ☀ 7.30am–
midnight Mon-Fri, 9.30am-
1pm Sat-Sun Ⓜ Monte
Napoleone

Il Coriandolo (3, B3)

Italiano Classico €€€
Like a little black dress, Il Coriandolo is the classic choice to accompany gallery openings or business meetings – and in the right company, it hints at other possibilities. The house spumante is a worthy prelude to house-made truffle ravioli with butter and crispy sage, whether you've come for a power lunch in a leather banquette or scintillating dinner conversation in the covered garden.

☎ 02 869 32 73 🖳 www
.ilcoriandolo.com ✉ Via
dell'Orso 1 ☀ 12noon-3pm
& 7-11pm daily Ⓜ Duomo

Il Salumaio di Montenapoleone (3, E3)

Runway Getaway €€
Prosecco (Veneto wine) and pesto linguine in an ivy-covered courtyard surrounded by Gucci, Stella McCartney and Dior: yep, you're in Milan. Enjoy your *arugula* (rocket) salad among models trying not to look bored by their banker husbands, and get envious glances with the decadent tiramisu.

☎ 02 760 01 123 🖳 www
.ilsalumaiodimontenapoleone
.it (in Italian) ✉ Via Monte
Napoleone ☀ 11am-7.30pm
Mon-Fri Ⓜ San Babila

Il Teatro (3, E2)

Slow Food €€€€
Slow and steady wins gourmet glory for this slow food restaurant, which brings bounties of artisanal cheeses, wines and other regional specialities to the table. Recently Sicilian cuisine brought down the house with a seven-course €100 tasting menu including tuna salami, Sicilian fish couscous, Modica chocolate eggplant ratatouille and Palermo lemon sorbet.

☎ 02 77 088 ✉ Via Gesú,
6/8 ☀ 7.30-11pm Mon-Sat
Ⓜ Monte Napoleone

BRRRUNCH

For shopaholics in momentary remission and late-night revellers rudely awoken by church bells, this American-inspired trend (pronounced with a rolling Italian R) is an indispensable prelude to museums. But no matter how loudly your stomach is growling, don't neglect the fine print – most prix-fixe brunches run €20 to €30, depending how many dishes and drinks are included. Here are some of the hottest brunch spots in the centre, near museums:

Art Café (3, B1; ☎ 02 805 36 12; Via Brera 23; Ⓜ Lanza) Right across the jammed sidewalk from Bar Jamaica. You may not think you're hungry after last night, but smell that à la carte gnocchi or tortellini, and then we'll talk.

Bar Jamaica (3, C1; ☎ 02 87 67 23; Via Brera 32; Ⓜ Lanza) One of the few places serving brunch dishes made to order, à la carte. Get here early if you want a sidewalk seat and house special pasta – they're long gone by 1.30pm.

Straf Bar (3, D4; ☎ 02 80 50 81; Via San Raffaele 3; Ⓜ Duomo) For €22, you too can make like a fashionista, plunk a cushion from the bar on the sidewalk, and enjoy omelettes and strawberries in sunglasses.

Italian Bar (3, B4)

Peckish for Lunch €€

Flattery will get you everywhere at Peck's blush-pink lunch bistro that gives everyone a nice healthy glow, with help from superb wines by the glass. The wait staff all in bow ties will be pleased to recommend a Barolo to accompany your tortellini Peck and *bresaola* (dried salted beef) with *arugula*, capers, oil and lemon.
☎ 02 869 30 17
🖳 www.peck.it ✉ Via Cesare Cantù 3 ⊙ 7.30am-8.30pm Mon-Sat Ⓜ Duomo

Luini (3, D4)

Pocket Pastries for Pocket Change €

Stockbrokers and student radicals, models and their harried hairdressers might get together here and sing *Kumbaya*, if they didn't all have their mouths full. *Panzerotti* is Milanese for yummy at this popular purveyor of pizza-dough pastries stuffed with cheeses, spinach, tomato, pesto and prosciutto.
☎ 02 864 61 917 🖳 www .luini.it ✉ Via Santa Radegonda 16 ⊙ 7am-8pm Mon-Sat Ⓜ Duomo

Dine out in Milanese style

Nobu (3, D2)

Globetrotting Sushi €€€€

A dozen years and as many restaurants later, chef Nobuyuki Matsuhisa still mixes continents and cuisines with whimsical flair, as though a lovesick slab of *hamo* sashimi might return from a rainy weekend in Paris drenched in foie gras, before it faints in a puddle of truffle oil on your plate. The prices and the people-watching are better in the sultry bar downstairs, where the orange glow turns men wearing bronzer into Oompa Loompas.
☎ 02 623 12 645 ✉ Via Pisoni 1 ⊙ 5pm-midnight Mon, noon-3pm & 5pm-midnight Tue-Sat, closed Sun & Aug Ⓜ Monte Napoleone

Paper Moon (3, F4)

Primo Primi €€

Lust for labels may have brought you to Quadrilatero d'Oro, but this house-made tagliolini with shrimp and zucchini blossoms may inspire you to take up permanent residence. If you can get past the *primi* (first courses) and the wood-fired pizzas, try the heartbreakingly tender carpaccio with *arugula* and *grana padano* cheese with the sprightly white Vernaccia.
☎ 02 79 60 83 ✉ Via Bagutta 1 ⊙ noon-3pm & 7-11pm Ⓜ San Babila

---

MORE POWER TO YOU

Power-lunching is a way of life in Milan, since the city's many commuters don't have enough time to head home for the traditional *pranzo* (lunch) and *pausa* (siesta). Prices downtown are not much less for lunch than for dinner, but there may be a fixed-price lunch special. Here's where to take which lunch guests to make a good impression:

Bagutta Business people who secretly want to be fashion designers.

Il Coriandolo Contemporary art dealers who personally prefer da Vinci.

Italian Bar Prospective in-laws and anyone else that needs plying with wine.

La Brisa Suits with sunglasses propped up on their foreheads.

Le Vigne Six of your closest friends (it's that reasonable).

Taverna degli Amici Fashion designers who secretly want to be business people.

Pattini & Marinoni (3, B1)
Really Good Baked Goods €
Non-stop, hot-out-of-the-oven action for under €3. Weekdays the wood bar is lined with working stiffs, ties tossed over one shoulder and hair tucked behind ears to dive into house-made pasta. After 9pm, art students and aperitivi revellers amble in for tomato and green olive foccacia, only to return hungover the next morning for brioches.
☎ 02 805 30 96 ⊠ Via Solferino 5 ☾ 7am-2am Mon-Sat Ⓜ Lanza

Ristorante Bagutta (3, E3)
Tuscany Meets Lombardy for Lunch €€€
The Ministry of Cultural Resources calls Bagutta a historical landmark, but your taste buds will call it fabulous: the toothsome lamb chops with sage and the melt-away spinach gnocchi with gorgonzola have kept napkins expectantly tucked under chins here since 1920.
☎ 02 760 00 902 ⊠ Via Bagutta 14 ☾ noon-3pm, 7pm-midnight Mon-Sat Ⓜ San Babila

NORTH

Ex Mauri (2, C2)
Venetian with Milanese Verve €€
If haute cuisine ever climbed down off its pedestal and ran off with a roguish Venetian osteria, their love child would be Ex Mauri. Pull up a school chair at a lovingly scuffed table for imaginative Venetian-inspired seafood and desserts made in-house – including dreamy lemon gelato.
☎ 02 608 56 028 ⌨ www .exmauri.com ⊠ Via

Federico Confalonieri 5 ☾ Closed Sunday and Saturday lunch Ⓜ Garibaldi

Latteria San Marco (2, C3)
Dairy Do €€
Lactose intolerance is simply not an option when confronted with the choice of tangy fusilli with herbed ricotta and spring onions, or savoury *faro* (spelt) with *mozzarella di bufala* (buffalo mozzarella cheese) and fresh tomatoes. The house menu changes daily, featuring homemade dishes with seasonal ingredients and organic wines.
☎ 02 659 76 53 ⊠ Via San Marco 24 ☾ 12.30-2.30pm, 7.30-10pm Mon-Fri Ⓜ Moscova

Princi (2, C2)
Delicious by Design Bakery €
Do baked goods taste better served on a black stone counter with a canal flowing through it? Avant-garde architect Claudio Silvestrin thought so, and you'll be inclined to agree while devouring your flaky apple strudel or foccacia slathered with fontina cheese and prosciutto.
☎ 02 290 60 832 ⌨ www .princi.it ⊠ Piazza XXV Aprile 5 ☾ 6am-midnight daily Ⓜ Moscova

Ristorante Solferino (2, C2)
Timeless Milanese €€
Salivary glands have worked overtime here for a century, thanks to hearty classics like osso bucco swathed in risotto, unexpected delights like fish tortelloni, and an extensive vegetarian menu. Join Italian film stars risking their girlish figures with the

in-house pastry chef's creations, and journalists steadily losing their objectivity over a superior wine selection.
☎ 02 290 05748 ⌨ www .ilsolferino.com ⊠ Via Castelfidardo 2 Ⓜ Moscova

Teatro7 (2, C1)
Fusion with Theatrical Flair €€€
Dinner theatre takes on new meaning with a web cam and open kitchen revealing three chefs at work on fusion creations, road-testing cutting-edge kitchen technology. Audience participation night is Tuesday, when diners cook their own gourmet meals under a chef's guidance – in Italian, with self-explanatory hand gestures.
☎ 02 699 00 72 ⌨ www .teatro7.com ⊠ Via Civerchio 9 ☾ lunch 12-2.30pm Mon-Fri, dinner 8-11pm Wed-Sun, cooking school Tue Ⓜ Zara

SOUTH

Anadima (2, B6)
Easy-to-please Milanese €€
Prozac is no match for 40 *bocconi perfetti* (perfect bites) of cold cuts and cheeses, 60 varieties of wine, and a serotonin-laced hot-pepper-chocolate soufflé. The manic pink and green pop-art décor looks on the bright side of every day or night by the Navigli, and the kitchen stays open until 1.30am.
☎ 02 832 19 81 ⊠ Via Pavia 10 ☾ 8.30am-3pm Tue-Sat, 5.30pm-2am Tue-Sun
🚋 3, 15 Ⓜ Porta Genova

Bar della Crocetta (2, D5)
Impressive Panini €
Think sandwiches are nothing to write home about? Get ready to break out those

postcards once you pick from the seven-page (!) menu of marvellous *panini* (grilled sandwiches), from the *Alé* (salami, prosciutto, scamorza cheese, arugula, hearts of palm) to the *Zia* (bresaola, fresh mozzarella, tomato, lettuce).
☎ 02 545 02 28 ✉ Corso di Porta Romana 67 (at Metro stop) ☯ 9am-2am Mon-Sat Ⓜ Crocetta

Be Bop (2, C6)
Pizza with Pizzazz €€
Forget Chianti-bottle candelabras and year-round Christmas lights – this pizzeria is pure Milan style,

with a tree growing in a glass box in the middle of the restaurant, salvaged wood flooring paving the walls and lighting that'll make a model of you yet. Go with the classic *mozzarella di buffala* pizza with fresh tomatoes, followed by dense, intense chocolate salami.
☎ 02 837 69 72 ✉ Col di Lana 4 ☯ 12.30-2.30pm & 7.30-10.30pm daily 🚋 3, 15 Ⓜ Porta Genova

Fingers (2, E6)
Multilingual Fish €€€
When Brazilian chefs and Italian restauranters get together in Milan, they

make sushi and beautiful music together. This trendy tatami-matted ristorante does a brisk trade in Italian carpaccio/sushi and squid ink risotto to Nobu defectors wanting less attitude and more food for their money.
☎ 02 541 22 675 ✉ Via S Gerolamo Emiliani 2 ☯ 8pm-midnight Tue-Sun Ⓜ Lodi

Giulio Pane e Ojo (2, E6)
Roman Conquest €€
If all the Roman restaurants in town were this winsome, Milan would probably start calling itself Mediolanum again. The wait staff dish up

BEEN THERE, DRANK THAT: LOMBARD WINES
Franciacorta DOCG The breakout star of Lombard wines, this sparkling white is a relative newcomer developed in the 1950s using the French *methode champenoise*. Today no upscale Milanese menu could do without it, and it's one of a couple dozen Italian wines awarded the DOCG quality denomination (a cut above esteemed DOC).
Lambrusco Mantovano DOC Rules were made to be broken by this light-hearted and slightly fizzy (yes, fizzy) red, a Milanese favourite for more than a millennium.
Lugana DOC Fine seafood demands a little something extra, and this underappreciated charmer from Lombardy's border with the Veneto brings crisp flair to the table.
Oltrepó Pavese Barbera DOC Riots broke out in the Middle Ages when Milan was cut off from Oltrepó, Lombardy's most renowned wine region. You'll relate when you sip this rousing Barbera, a must with rich Milanese dishes like osso bucco.
Valtellina DOCG Like your favourite dinner guests, this red has a dry, distinctive wit that pairs well with meats without being too forward – da Vinci loved the stuff.

Sample fusion dishes incorporating Milanese culinary flair

Roman sass when asked to help you choose between the *bucatini amatriciana* (tube pasta with tomato, pecorino and pig's cheek) and *saltimbocca* (veal with sage and bacon). At these prices, puh-lease – you can't lose.

☎ 02 545 61 89 💻 www .giuliopaneojo.com ✉ Via Muratori 10 🕑 7.30pm-1am daily Ⓜ Porta Romana

Le Vigne (2, B6)

Honest Osteria €€
Blindfold yourself and point at the menu, because that's the only way to choose among zucchini flowers stuffed with artisanal herbed ricotta, risotto with shrimp and nasturtium flowers, and a salad of octopus, artichoke and zucchini. Get them all with a glass or two of the house wine and enjoy the stupor of the culinarily blessed.

☎ 02 837 56 17 ✉ Ripa di Porta Ticinese 61 🕑 noon-3pm & 7-11pm Mon-Sat Ⓜ Porta Genova

Luca e Andrea Café-Bar (2, B6)

Picturesque Pasta €
An embarrassment of riches at starving-artist prices, with generous pasta and risotto specials served canalside. The gnocchi with gorgonzola washed down with a quarter-carafe of the house red could inspire your next performance art piece, if you could only move off your chair.

☎ 02 581 01 142 ✉ Alzaia Naviglio Grande 34 🕑 noon-3pm & 5-11pm Mon-Sat Ⓜ Porta Genova

Osteria del Binari (2,B5)

Welcome to the Family
Food €€
Crashing an Italian wedding is the only other way you'd come by such heaping platters of handmade pasta, select cuts of meat and home-baked pastries. With Tuscan wine and loved ones gathered around, someone's bound to feel a toast coming on – quick, duck out back and join the lawn bowling already in progress.

☎ 02 894 06 753 ✉ Via Tortona 1 🕑 7-11pm Mon-Sat Ⓜ Porta Genova

Sadler (2, B6)

Creative Classics €€€€
The Biblioteca Ambrosiana of Milanese haute cuisine delivers higher education for the palate, with glassed-in bookcases of rare wines and comfy chairs for serious cram sessions. Get wise to scampi with quail eggs and caviar, lobster with polenta gnocchi, or classes (in Italian) with Claudio Sadler by prior arrangement.

☎ 02 581 04451 💻 www .sadler.it ✉ Via Troilo 14 at Via Conchetta 🕑 7-11.30pm Mon-Tue, closed August and first two weeks of January 🚃 3, 15 Ⓜ Porta Genova

EAST

Anna & Leo (2, F1)

Seafood Surprise €
Contrary to popular Milanese myth, a delightful seafood dinner is not inevitably followed by a bill that leaves you gasping like a fish out of water. Pull up a seat in the garden and enjoy the company of local art gallerists, pleasant service, pasta for under €6 and fish under €7.

☎ 02 215 73 09 ✉ Via Conte Rosso 28 🕑 7-11pm Mon-Sat Ⓜ Lambrate

Joia (2, D3)

Milan au Naturel €€€€
After one too many servings of leaden *cotoletta alla Milanese*, you'll be jumping for (all together now) Joia, thanks to chef Pietro Leeman's way with fresh vegetables and light, clean flavours. Vegetarians have choices here that strip away the meat stock (what, you thought rich Milanese risotto was vegetarian?), though even vegans may be tempted by the artisanal cheese plate.

☎ 02 295 22 124 💻 www .joia.it ✉ Via Panfilo Castaldi 18 🕑 noon-2.30pm & 7.30pm-midnight Mon-Fri, 7.30pm-midnight Sat Ⓜ Porta Venezia

Pizzeria Spontini (2, E2)

Pizza by the Slice €
A hot slice isn't a fall back but a first-rate choice at this wood-fired pizza joint. The

frosted-glass and chrome décor may be new, but traditionalists need have no fear: this is the same pizza dough recipe responsible for rejuvenating Corso Buenos Aires shoppers since 1953.
☎ 02 204 74 44 ⊠ Via Gaspare Spontini ◷ 11.45am-2:15pm & 6-11.30pm Tue-Sun Ⓜ Lima

Taverna degli Amici (2, E5)
Grill with Style €€
Expandable waistbands are going to be all the rage next season, if the eating habits of the fashion designers thronging the Amici are any indication. Prada, Etro, and Costume National converge here for lunch, and only naïve students from the nearby Design Institute choose the

wan salad bar over the great grilled meats.
☎ 02 551 94 005 ⊠ Via Spartaco 4 ◷ noon-2.30pm & 7-11pm Mon-Fri, 7-11pm Sat Ⓜ Porta Romana

WEST

Antica Trattoria della Pesa (2, C2)
Memorable Milanese €€€
A Milanese recipe for instant nostalgia: Take the landmark building where Ho Chi Minh stayed in the 1930s, add literary types from nearby Mondadori and Rizzoli publishing houses, mix with Milanese comfort food and plenty of wine, then finish with *tarte tatin* that would make Marcel Proust weep. Repeat as necessary.

☎ 02 655 57 41 ⊠ Viale Pasubio 10 ◷ 12.30-2.30pm, 7.30-11pm daily Ⓜ Cairoli

Da Martino (2, C2)
Steak & Then Some €€
Get that new suit taken out if you must, but do not miss the Florentine steak at Da Martino. The three-inch-thick hunk of grass-fed beast arrives at your table with the bone still in, then carved with all due ceremony. Devour it with a side of roasted rosemary potatoes, but leave room for surprisingly avant-garde *panna cotta* with almonds and sour cherries.
☎ 02 655 49 74 ⊠ Via Carlo Farini 8 ◷ 7-11pm Mon-Tue & Thu-Sun Ⓜ Garibaldi

CAFFÉ CULTURE

Sure, you could toss back an espresso at almost any coffee bar in Milano for under a Euro, but these places are worth paying double or triple for table service.

Armani Jeans Caffé (2, C5; ☎ 02 833 90 062; Via Vetere 6 Ⓜ Porta Genova) Fiera architect Massimiliano Fuksas draped this place in PVC, creating a glossy blue bar and all-red courtyard café to restore that rosy glow to your cheeks.

Caffé Cova (3, E3; ☎ 02 760 05 578; Via Monte Napoleone 8 Ⓜ Monte Napoleone) If you've resisted the temptation to max out your credit card thus far, celebrate with a glass of Cova's own label prosecco.

Gucci Caffé (3, C4; ☎ 02 859 79 91; Galleria Vittorio Emmanuele II Ⓜ Duomo) Take your tea overlooking the Galleria with logoed Gucci chocolates, or a light lunch of quiches, muffins and pastries for €12.

Just Cavalli Bar (3, E2; ☎ 02 763 90 893; Via della Spiga 30 Ⓜ Monte Napoleone) Take the glass pod elevator to the subterranean café lined with fish tanks, attended by blindingly handsome wait staff who may yet succeed in reviving manly ponytails.

Mediateca Bookshop e Caffetteria (2, D3; ☎ 02 365 27 326; Via della Moscova 28 Ⓜ Moscova) Emerging film makers banter and flirt unedited for hours in this sunny, glassed-in courtyard.

The Photographers Caffé (2, C3; ☎ 02 885 52 073; Via Legano 4 Ⓜ Lanza) Flop down on a leather couch with a *caffé corretto* (liquor-spiked coffee), and decide which of the photographs by noted local artists you'd like to take home – at these prices, take two.

Zucca in Galleria (3, C4; ☎ 02 864 64 435; Galleria Vittorio Emanuele II Ⓜ Duomo) Breakfast and coffee in this swanky, historic Liberty-style joint will cost you, but the people-watching is a bargain at any price.

La Brisa (2, C4)

Leisurely Lunch €€€

Whether you've come to this garden hideaway for work or play is irrelevant, because once the tenderloin with pomegranate seeds and *arugula* arrives, it's pure pleasure. Watch as Lombard wines loosen the power ties of fellow patrons here with the €20 fixed-price lunch – or better yet, join in.
☎ 02 864 50 521 ✉ Via Brisa 15 🕑 noon-2.30pm & 7-11pm Mon-Fri & 7-11pm Sun Ⓜ Cairoli

Serendib (2, C2)

Sri Lankan €€

Maybe it's fate, but you can call it (wait for it) serendibity to find this first-rate Sri Lankan restaurant just when you were in the mood for something hot and cheap that hasn't served time as a spokesmodel on Italian television. Vegetarians can rejoice at the hearty lentil and stewed vegetable options, while *kukulmas* (marinated chicken) is crowd-pleasing poultry.

☎ 02 659 21 39 🖳 www .serendib.it ✉ Via Pontida 2 🕑 7-11pm Tue-Sun Ⓜ Moscova

WORTH A TRIP

Il Luogo di Aimo e Nadia

Versatile Milanese €€€€

Milanese like their food like they like their clothes: artful, inventive, in season and suitable for any occasion. No wonder everyone adores Aimo and Nadia Moroni's

Artful food at Il Luogo di Aimo e Nadia

place, with memorable seasonal fare like fresh tagliolini pasta with truffles and turnips in winter, pistachio-encrusted prawns with artichokes for spring and a wine list that won't quit year-round.
☎ 02 41 68 86 🖳 www .aimoenadia.com ✉ Via Montecuccoli 6 (2km off Map 2) 🕑 noon-2.30pm & 7.30-11.30pm Mon-Fri, 7.30-11.30pm Sat, closed August Ⓜ Bande Nere

WHERE TO GO FOR GELATO

No Milanese neighbourhood would be complete without at least one *gelateria* (ice cream parlour). Here's where to find the ideal *cono* (cone) with two flavours and optional *panna* (whipped cream):

North: L'Angolo della Moscova Caffeteria (2, C3; ☎ 02 365 62 887; Via della Moscova 29 Ⓜ Moscova) Celebrate your birthday early with classic flavours like *zabaglione* (egg cream) and *amarena* (sour cherry) shaped into flowers.

South: Rivareno (2, C6; ☎ 02 890 77 147; Viale Col di Lana 8 Ⓜ Porta Genova) Savour creamy goodness made from superior ingredients – Dutch red cocoa, Madagascar vanilla, hazelnuts toasted to perfection – and surf the internet for free too.

East: Da Carmelo (2, F1; Viale delle Rimembranze, Ⓜ Lambrate) Genuine Sicilian gelato, made in-house by Sicilian-born Carmelo, the guy who's scooping your cone; his lemon is the best in the city, if not the planet.

West: Chocolat (2, B4; ☎ 02 481 00 597; Via Boccaccio 9 Ⓜ Cadorna) The ultra-rich *cioccolato pepperoncino* (hot pepper chocolate) will give your tastebuds the best case of hypothermia ever.

Entertainment

There's no such thing as bad timing for good times in Milan: the calendar of events never stops year-round (see p60), and bars run seven days a week from 10pm until around 3am or 4am. Milan is a social butterfly that spreads its wings after dark, flitting from happy hour to avant-garde theatre and late-night clubs with unabashed glee and unmistakable style. Keep up if you dare at the venues listed in this chapter, or featured in Milan's many free culture-vulture magazines and event listings (p87).

APERITIVO BARS

Milan may not have invented happy hour, but it surely perfected the concept. Milan's aperitivi bars stretch that insufficient hour with unattractive drink specials into a two or three hour ritual between 6pm and 9pm, when a €5 to €8 cocktail, glass of wine, or beer comes with unlimited access to a buffet of antipasti, bruschetta, cold cuts, salads, even seafood and pasta. Most bars and restaurants offer aperitivi, but Milan's best buffets are singled out here.

Aperitivo bars – a Milanese evening ritual

Bar Jamaica (3, C1)

If the Jamaica's bulletin board could, it would surely groan under the weight of notices pinned to it by artists and film makers advertising their latest projects – the inspiration for which probably came from a late night right on these premises. Art students from nearby Accademia di Brera nurse drinks for days on coveted sidewalk seats, but the covered patio is a good bet.
☎ 02 87 67 23 ✉ Via Brera 32 ☽ 8am-2am Mon-Sat, 8am-8.30pm Sun Ⓜ Lanza

Bhangra Bar (2, B3)

Hip Milanese like their bars like they like their cuisine: geographically vague and otherwise distinctive. Bhangra Bar delivers on both counts with a couscous-and-curry aperitivo buffet, served with a side of African percussion on Fridays, international beats on 'Melting Pot' Thursdays, and trip-hop plus a free shiatsu massage with our €5.50 drink on 'Tao' Sundays.
☎ 02 349 34 469 💻 www .bhangrabarmilano.com ✉ Piazza Sempione 1 ☽ 7pm-midnight Wed, 7-11pm Thu, 7.30pm-2am Fri, 10pm-2am Sat, 8-10pm Sun Ⓜ Cadorna

Café Marino alla Scala (3, C3)

Every detail here seems scientifically calculated to distract from the demands of the day: the lavish spread with fresh seafood and organic ingredients, harried but charming bartenders, and a wall-sized video art piece playing in a loop behind a Milanese ensemble cast of business moguls and classical musicians, fashionistas and famished students. Bottle that formula: it works.

☎ 02 864 51 580
✉ Piazza della Scala 5
🕑 8am-1am Mon-Sat &
8pm-1am Sun
Ⓜ Duomo

Cantine Isola (2, B2)
Only octogenarians make use
of the sole table in back –
everyone else hovers near
the bar, balancing plates of

bruschetta and holding glasses
at the ready for when the
in-house sommelier gives the
nod to open a fine vintage
Barbera. The selection of wines

SPECIAL EVENTS
For fashion-related events, see Catwalk Calendar (p42).

Year-round *Le Voci della Citta* – 'The Voices of the City' concert series, held in Milan's historic churches; see tourist office (p89) for calendar listings

January *Corteo dei Re Magi* – Milan's traditional Nativity procession

February *Carnevale Ambrosian* – the world's longest carnival, culminates with a parade to the Duomo

Stramilano (🖥 www.stramilano.it) – half-marathon from Castello Sforzesco to the arena

March *Milano Internazionale Antiquariato* – the four-day international antiques show held in the Fiera di Milano

MiArt (🖥 www.fmi.it/miart) – contemporary art fair held in the Fiera di Milano

April *Salone Internazionale del Mobile* – International Furniture Fair held in Nuova Fiera di Milano Rho-Pero (p27)

Milano International Fine Art & Antiques Show – one of Italy's biggest collector events

May *Mille Miglia* – when classic cars race from Brescia (near Milan) to Rome and back

June *Festa del Naviglio* – with music, food and special events the first 10 days of June

International Gay & Lesbian Milan Film Festival (🖥 www.cinemagaylesbico.com) – five days of film with gay/les/bi/trans themes

Milanesiana Literature, Music, Cinema Festival – three weeks of cultural events citywide

Notte Bianca – stay up all night with the rest of Milan the third Saturday in June, when concerts, performances and spontaneous spectacles erupt all over the city like fireworks

June–September *Serate Al Museo* (🖥 www.comune.milano.it/museiemostre) – concerts held in Milan museums

July–August *Latin American Festival* (🖥 www.latino americando.it) – events celebrating Latin America in Milan

September *Rock in Idro* (🖥 www.rockinidro.com) – brings international indie rock to the Idroscalo

Italian Grand Prix (🖥 www.monzanet.it) – at the Monza autodrome outside Milan

Football season – kicks off at San Siro Stadium (p21)

Milano Film Festival (☎ 02 713 613; 🖥 www.milanofilmfestival.it) – Ten days of features, shorts, open-air screenings and more at Castello Sforzesco

October *Milan City Marathon* (🖥 www.milanocitymarathon.it) starts at Porta Venezia and loops around the city and the Navigli to the Duomo

Festival del Teatro del Mediterraneo – begins with three months of theatre from Mediterranean countries

Concert and theatre season – begins citywide

November *Milan Jazz Festival* – see tourist office (p89) for calendar listings

Startmilano (🖥 www.start-mi.net) Milan's newest contemporary art showcase

December *Festa di Sant'Ambrogio* (7 December) – celebrations honouring Milan's patron saint

Opera season – begins at La Scala

from 400 exceptional vintners is an education in a glass, so you'll leave wiser and drunker.
☎ 02 331 52 49 ✉ Via Paolo Sarpi 30 ⏰ 10am-9pm Tue-Sun Ⓜ Garibaldi

Da Claudio (3 B2)
Fishmonger by day, Claudio is Nobu's archrival by night. Once the floors are hosed down, corks pop and crowds arrive for spumante and a sampler plate of the sliced *carpaccio* (raw) catch of the day (€10). This Milan-style sushi is drizzled with extra virgin olive oil, pepper and lemon atop raddichio, and served with crusty bread instead of rice.
☎ 02 805 68 57 ✉ Via Ponte Vetero 16 ⏰ 6-9pm Wed-Sat Ⓜ Cairoli

Diana Garden (2, E3)
Reel around the fountain in the lush gardens of this Art Nouveau palazzo, cocktail in hand: you'll have plenty of stylish company. Even with the crowds here, the staff never forgets a drink order and there's usually a plush seat to be found indoors.
☎ 02 205 82 081 ✉ Viale Piave 42 ⏰ 10am-2am daily, garden 5-11pm spring/summer Ⓜ Porta Venezia

El Brellin (2, B6)
The ancient mill on the side of the building serves no modern purpose other than to raise the old-world charm of this canalside spot to irresistible levels, and the drinks are reliable even if the buffet is limited to light salads.
☎ 02 581 01 351 ✉ Alzaia Naviglio Grande 14 ⏰ 12.30-2.30pm & 7.30pm-1am Mon-Sat, 12-3pm Sun Ⓜ Porta Genova

Le Biciclette (2, B5)
This one-time bike warehouse must have stored up great karma in its prior existence to be reincarnated as one of the best aperitivi bars in Milan. A combination of luck and earliness will snag you a coveted baroque couch with glassed-in bicycle memorabilia underfoot, and first pick of the dishes crowding the bar.
☎ 02 581 04 325 🖥 www.lebiciclette.com ✉ Via Torti 4 ⏰ 6pm-2am Mon-Sat & 12.30-2pm Sun Ⓜ Sant'Ambrogio

L'Elephante (2, E3)
The expert bartender here is happiest when mixing things up and the same can be said of the alternative-trendy

crowd, which tends toward lesbian-and-gay-friendly, bi-curious or generically open-minded. The setting is equally eclectic: no two chairs are alike and the snack buffet is plenty varied.
☎ 02 295 18 768 ✉ Via Melzo 22 ⏰ 6.30pm-2am Ⓜ Porta Venezia

Living (2, B3)
Score an armchair at this former post office before 7pm and after a couple of cocktails with your choice of 100 kinds of vodka, they may have to fold you up and mail you home. Enjoy the vast buffet, but don't leave your seat for long – the wait for another cushy spot is longer than post office queues at Christmas.
☎ 02 331 00 824 🖥 www.livingmilano.com ✉ Piazza Sempione 2 ⏰ noon-3pm & 6pm-2am Tue-Sun Ⓜ Lanza

Noy (2, A4)
Only in Milan could a garage find divine inspiration. The almighty bar fills the void where a truck might once have been, and leather armchairs clustered convivially around tables are haloed in light from skylights in the corrugated roof above. Drop by for brunch

Children playing the part at Milan's lively Carnevale Ambrosian

or aperitivi after a heavenly wellness treatment at Habits Culti (p31) next door.
☎ 02 481 10 375 ✉ Via Soresina 4 ☯ 8am-2am Tue-Sun Ⓜ Pagano

Shu (2, C5)
The mothership has landed and it's a great place for a drink. Two monumental gold arms support a green ceiling with a matrix of circuitry and box lights like a motherboard from Jupiter. Pull up a frosted glass chair and tuck into your tuna tartare and eggplant-scampi *timabllo* (casserole) before you're beamed up or happy hour ends, whichever comes first.
☎ 02 583 15 720 🖥 www .shumilano.it ✉ cnr Via Molino delle Armi & Via della Chiusa ☯ 6pm-2am nightly Ⓜ Missori

Yguana (2, C5)
It's a jungle out there during happy hour, when trailblazers lead expeditions to the packed buffet and back out to coveted kerbside wicker chairs. Head to the rainforest-themed balcony, where seats aren't such an endangered species.
☎ 02 894 04195 ✉ Via Papa Gregorio XIV 6 ☯ 6-11pm Tue-Sat Ⓜ Missori

BARS

Atomic Bar (2, D2)
Like hanging out inside a lava lamp, with vintage vinyl sofas and faux-fur chairs in molten shapes, and walls splashed with psychedelic patterns and mesmerising glitter. Settle into rare grooves from the '60s and '70s on Sunday, then let it all bubble up and over the top on gay-friendly 'Drama Queen' Fridays.
☎ 33 414 77 164 🖥 www .atomicbar.it ✉ Via Felice Casati 24 ☯ 10pm-3am Ⓜ Repubblica

Bar Magenta (2, B4)
Grab a kerbside seat here, and let Milan come to you.

Locals drift in for espresso, sandwiches and beer; students show up around 5pm to stake out spots near the buffet; models saunter in around 7pm, pretending not to be hungry and eating from everyone else's plates. Bartop antics in abbreviated clothing draw perverts and trainwreck-watchers on 'Coyote Ugly' Thursdays.
☎ 02 805 38 08 ✉ Via Giosué Carducci 13 ☯ 9am-2am Ⓜ Cadorna

Boccascena Café (2, B4)
The scene is set at an 18th century palazzo, with a charming courtyard and clocktower. Actors, and artists mill around tables, anticipating or reviewing the evening's entertainment at Teatro Litta indoors. In the Teatro's grand foyer, drinks are presented with a flourish and dramatically lit by mod chrome chandeliers. Unscripted dialogue and much levity ensues; the end is entirely up to you.

DINNER & DANCING

Make an evening of it at these dinner-plus venues:

4cento (2, C6; ☎ 02 895 17 771; Via Campazzino 14 ☯ 8pm-6am Tue-Sun) Sprawl out on cushions and mats for a fusion feast and your knees will probably creak when you stand up to get your groove on after dinner – but by 6am closing time, you'll be plenty limber.

Galleria Meravigli (3, B4; ☎ 02 805 51 25; Via Meravigli 3 ☯ closed Sun Ⓜ Cordusio) Build your strength with the happy hour buffet in the Liberty-style arcade, then rest on a divan with a *mojito* (minty Cuban cocktail) 'til tango classes begin.

La Banque (3, B4; ☎ 02 869 96 565; Via B Porrone 6 ☯ 6pm-2am Tue-Thu, 6pm-4am Fri-Sat, 7pm-midnight Sun, closed Aug Ⓜ Duomo) Ties and tongues get progressively looser as happy hour devolves into dinner – and once dancing kicks in around 10pm, you never know where they'll end up.

Picanha (2, A3; ☎ 02 392 14 408; Piazzale Lotto 14 Ⓜ Lotto) First the antipasti buffet appears, then out come giant skewers of succulent grilled meats and pineapple, and just when movement of any kind seems impossible, the live samba propels you to the dance floor.

Bar-hop through the Brera district

☎ 02 805 58 82 ✉ Teatro Litta, Corso Magenta 24 ⏰ 10am-4pm Mon, 10am-late Tue-Fri, 3pm-late Sat, 3-10pm Sun Ⓜ Cadorna

Cantiere dei Sensi (2, C2)
Let fine Italian design and wine go to your head at this showplace bar, where you can actually buy the newfangled wineglass you're drinking from, or that clever plate under your €25 set-price meal (including appetiser, wine, primo and coffee).
☎ 02 668 03 446 ✉ Via Carmagnola 5 ⏰ 8am-4pm & 6pm-1am Tue-Fri; 8.30pm-1.30am Sat; 8am-2.30pm & 8pm-12.30am Mon Ⓜ Garibaldi

Caruso (3, D2)
The living is good and the people-watching even better at this sidewalk café in Milan's most fashionable piazza, with the best-dressed parade hauling designer booty and little dogs along Via Manzoni, gingerly descending Montenapo Metro steps in staggering heels, and pretending not to be flustered by the pulchritude of Emporio Armani Caffé waiters.

☎ 02 72 31 41 ✉ Grand Hotel et de Milano, Via Croce Rossa ⏰ noon-midnight Tue-Sun Ⓜ Montenapoleone

Frida (2, C1)
No pretensions, no entourages, just good music, good value and good times. The jumble of tables outside and couches indoors make it easy to bond over beer, and the display of local emerging photographers is a handy conversation-starter with the arty alternative crowd. Come for live jazz Sundays and €5 happy hour 6.30pm to 9pm.
☎ 02 608 18 34 ✉ Via Pollaiuolo 3 ⏰ noon-2am Mon-Fri, 6.30pm-2am Sat-Sun Ⓜ Zara

G-Lounge (3, D5)
By day it's a hard-working lunch destination with a view of the Torre Velasca; by night it's a sultry lounge with a distinct flair for *caipirinhias* (minty Brazilian cocktails), mod Moroccan décor, and groovy chill-out music. Some call versatile G-Lounge a straight-friendly gay bar, others a gay-friendly straight bar – but you can just call it a fun night out in Milan.

☎ 02 805 30 42 ✉ Via Larga 8 ⏰ 7.30am-9.30pm Mon, 7.30am-2am Tue-Sun Ⓜ Duomo

Julien Lounge Bar (2, C3)
Get a manicure at the Julien Room across the street, and have a top-shelf cocktail in this upbeat chill-out lounge while they dry: it's every beauty buff's idea of the perfect lunch break. Girls' nights out begin with a Julien Room blow-out, happy hour here, then Just Cavalli or Old Fashion.
☎ 02 349 04 59 ✉ Via Carlo Maria Maggi 3/3 ⏰ noon-3pm, 6pm-1am Ⓜ Moscova

Light (2, C2)
All extraneous detail has been stripped away from this former woodworking factory, drawing your attention to exposed brick archways, fuchsia walls and the person glowing on the spotlit sofa next to you. The illuminated alabaster bar inspires a reverence usually reserved for altars, though you'll hardly see it for the aperitivi crowds in at 7pm.
☎ 02 626 90 631 ✉ Via Maroncelli 8 ⏰ 7pm-1am Ⓜ Garibaldi

Martini Bar (3, F3)

As seen through the bottom of your martini glass, these glossy black marble walls enclose a magical realm of Prince Charming waiters ruled by a gargantuan red jellyfish… oh wait, that's a chandelier, and this is Dolce & Gabbana. Have another and you'll be willing to forgive the tacky neon signage, if only because it won't stay in focus.

☎ 02 760 11 154 ⊠ Corso Venezia 15 ⏰ 10am-noon Tue & Fri; 10-7pm Wed, Thu & Sat Ⓜ San Babila

Roialto (2, A2)

Like an old-school movie star, this ruggedly handsome warehouse-turned-bar pretends to be unaware of its good looks. But there's no denying the appeal of those high ceilings, vintage leather club chairs, billiard tables and the wooden bar brought from Cuba – it's worth the lines and face patrol on weekends, and even returning to the scene of the crime for Sunday brunch.

☎ 02 349 36 616 ⊠ Via Piero della Francesca 55 ⏰ 6pm-2.30am Tue-Sat, 12.30-4pm & 6pm-2.30am Sun Ⓜ Lotto 🚃 1,14,19,33

Yar Bistrot (2, C5)

Once the pitchers (yes, pitchers) of vodka start pouring around 6pm, you'd better order some borsch and blinis; it's going to be another long, outrageous night at rococo Russian Yar. Tonight you're going to party like it's 1899, the Iron Curtain never went up or came down and men in fur coats weren't necessarily Italian fashion designers.

☎ 02 583 05 234 ⊠ Via G Mercalli 22 ⏰ 6pm-midnight Mon-Sat Ⓜ Crochetta

CLUBS

Gasoline Club (2, C2)

Everything seems larger than life in this small-scale disco, from the big dance moves to huge false eyelashes on Gay Tea Dance Sundays. Otherwise, manly attire ranges from designer tees and jeans

Cocktails: dusk 'til dawn

to black Speedos, while women dress to express. The bar is redecorated annually, in sometimes questionable taste – but the cocktails are beyond reproach.

☎ 02 339 774 57 97 🖥 www.discogasoline.it ⊠ Via Nino Bonnet 11a ⏰ 10.30pm-4am Thu-Sun, closed Aug Ⓜ Garibaldi

Gattopardo (2, A2)

Fashionable Milan worships at the altar of design by day, and at night recharges at this deconsecrated church with candles everywhere

WELCOME TO MILAN: PLEASE ADJUST YOUR GAYDAR

Milan is like the Bermuda Triangle for gaydar: anyone knows how to work a look, no-one plays to type, and on the right night, everyone's giving everyone else meaningful glances across crowded rooms. At least five nights a week, most clubs have a seamlessly mixed straight, gay and whatever clientele. Even at landmark gay/lesbian bars like Nuova Idea, L'Elephante and G-Lounge, most nights are straight-friendly.

Just to make things more unpredictable, at many clubs one night a week is designated as 'gay-friendly'. On these nights, men can wear whatever as long as they don their best skivvies, dirty dancing with scantily clad men becomes good clean fun for women, cross-dressing is to be expected and everyone flirts with the coat-check girl. For good times had by all, check out:

- Wednesday – Pervert at Hollywood (opposite)
- Thursday – Gossip at G-Lounge (p63)
- Friday – Jet Lag at Magazzini Generali (p66)
- Sunday – Gasoline Club's Gay Tea Dance (above) and Plastic (opposite)

HOT CHILD IN THE CITY

Warm weather turns Milan's parks into verdant living rooms where kids frolic all day, and adults take over at night. Enjoy balmy breezes and a stiff drink at these summer park venues, open May to September:

Bar Bianco (2, B3; ☎ 02 864 51 176; Parco Sempione, near arena; Ⓜ Lanza) The patio seats are fine for people-watching, but having drinks on the upper terrace amid the trees is like having a cocktail in a treehouse.

Just Cavalli Café (2, B3; ☎ 02 31 18 17 ✉ Parco Sempione at Torre Branca ⏱ 8pm-2am Ⓜ Cadorna) White tents bedecked with animal print create a burlesque carnival ride atmosphere under the Torre Branca – only to take this ride, you'll have to wink your way past the bouncers.

Lounge Paradise/Piscina Solari (2, A5; ☎ 02 469 52 78; Via Montevideo 20 ⏱ 6pm-12.30am summer only Ⓜ Sant'Agostino) Happy hour gets a whole lot happier when you're watching the sunset streak across the sky from a cushy lounge chair by the pool, with a buffet plate and cocktail for just €8.

Old Fashion Café (2, B3; ☎ 02 805 62 31 🖳 www.oldfashion.it ✉ Parco Sempione at the Triennale ⏱ 11pm-4am) Head straight for the disco on the enclosed back patio next to the Triennale, and provided the bouncers are suitably impressed, you can dance 'til the sun starts to rise over Parco Sempione.

and a bar where the altar once was. That mighty chandelier dangling from the cupola is mostly there for looks – but then the same can be said of the staff, and who's complaining?
☎ 02 345 37 699 ✉ Via Piero della Francesca 47 ⏱ 6pm-4am Tue-Sun Ⓜ Lotto 🚊 1,14,19,33

Hollywood (2, C2)
Bust out the glitter and limber up, because your gender is in for some bending among the glitterati, especially on 'Pervert' Wednesdays. Yes, this is the very club frequented by soccer players and supermodels, and if you stick around you might witness Milan's next scandal in the making – or be a party to it. What happens in Hollywood, stays in Milan.
☎ 02 659 89 96 ✉ Corso Como 15 ⏱ 10.30pm-4am Tue-Sun, closed Jul & Aug Ⓜ Garibaldi

Kineo (2, A2)
Cross a fashion week runway with a 1930s Cimitero Monumentale mausoleum, and you've got the perfect setting for high-drama drinks and devil-may-care disco. Lights dance around the room clad in floor-to-ceiling shiny black marble, though ultrasoft black leather banquettes make mobilising to the downstairs disco on weekends most challenging.
☎ 02 34 26 27 ✉ Via Piero della Francesca 54 ⏱ Tue-Sun Ⓜ Lotto 🚊 1,14,19,33

Nuova Idea (2, D2)
Go club-hopping without leaving this many-splendoured nightlife theme park, Milan's premier gay club since 1975. One room features ballroom dancing with an orchestra and tiaras galore; the next has cages with greased-up gogo dancers plying their trade in nosebleed-inducing heels.

At the centre of it all, Milan's most celebrated transvestites are constantly putting Fashion Week runways to shame.
⏱ 02 690 07 859 🖳 www.lanuovaidea.com ✉ Via Gaetano De Castillia 30 € €10 Fri & Sun, €16 Sat, Thu free with drink ⏱ 10.30pm-3am Thu-Sun Ⓜ Gioia

Plastic (2, F5)
How does Plastic keep throngs at the door six days a week, in a town as fickle about hot spots as footwear? Simple: strong drinks, fresh DJ line-ups each season, dim lighting and low seating to encourage a certain amount of groping. Saturdays are Bordello Night and Sundays are pan-sexual free-for-alls that make Studio 54 seem amateurish – go early, or face ruthless door selection after 9pm.
☎ 02 73 39 96 ✉ Viale Umbria 120 ⏱ 10pm-4am Tue-Sun, closed Aug Ⓜ Lodi

LIVE MUSIC

Le Trottoir (2, C6)
Party at your house – at least that's how it looks inside this former toll house, with art on the stairway, funky frescos and the inevitable cluster of artists attempting to discuss video art over the joyous din of a swinging ska band. That's right: that dinky raised platform is a stage, showcasing local alternative bands that get the whole place gyrating.
☎ 02 837 81 66 ✉ Piazza XXIV Maggio ◷ 11am-3am

An aural feast at a street cafe

Magazzini Generali (2, D6)
When an entire former warehouse full of people is working up a sweat to indie international acts, cutting-edge DJs and the best local bands, there's no cooler place to be in Milan. Can't argue with the price, either: most acts are under €15, there's free entry Wednesday, aka Night of Contemporary Beat, and the legendary Jet Lag Fridays are free with a drink.
☎ 02 552 11 313 ✉ Via Pietrasanta 14 ◷ 10pm-4am Wed-Sun, closed Jul & Aug Ⓜ Lodi

Rolling Stone (2, F4)
Belle and Sebastian, Arctic Monkeys, the Yeah Yeah Yeahs and a bunch of local bands you never heard of (but should) play Milan's leading rock venue. Patrons have been known to shower bands with adoration and contempt by spraying them with beer from the bar above the stage, but nowadays management is keeping an eye out for amp-destroying rabble-rousers (you know who you are).
☎ 02 73 31 72 ✉ Corso XXII Marzo 32 ◷ 10pm-3am Thu-Sat Ⓜ Porta Romana

Scimmie (2, B6)
Where else could you find a historic canalside pizzeria that puts on 363 live shows a year – only in Milan, baby. Jazz, alternative rock and blues are the strong suits of the emerging talents who play to overflow crowds inside Scimmie, in the garden, and on its new Jazz Boat (with dinner, €35). Concerts start at 10pm, and €8 to €12 entry includes your first drink.
☎ 02 894 02 874 ✉ Via Cardinale Ascanio Sforza 49 ◷ 8pm-3am Mon-Sat Ⓜ Porta Genova

HAVE TICKET, WILL TRAVEL
With the exception of bands that play Magazzini Generali and Rolling Stone, most major international acts that 'play Milan' actually play venues outside the city. When you get your tickets, check details for specially organised shuttle buses to and from the show. Otherwise, this is how to reach the major stadium-band venues:

FilaForum (☎ 02 4885 71; www.filaforum.it; Via di Vittorio, Agasso; Ⓜ Romolo/Famagosto then shuttle bus)

PalaVobis and **Mazda Palace** (☎ 02 334 00 551; Viale Sant'Elia 33; Ⓜ Lampugnano, near San Siro stadium)

San Siro Stadium (2,A3; Via Piccolomini; Ⓜ Lotto)

Villa Arconati (☎ 02 3500 5501; Castellazzo di Bollate, 5km north of Milan)

WHERE TO BUY TICKETS

For performances from rock to opera and the odd rock opera, head to these ticket outlets:

Box Tickets (☎ 02 847 09 750; www.boxtickets.it)
Buscemi Dischi (☎ 02 80 41 03; www.buscemi.com)
Messaggerie Musicali (☎ 02 760 55 404)
Milano Concerti (☎ 02 487 02 726; www.milanoconcerti.it)
Ticket One (☎ 02 39 22 61 or toll-free 840 052 720; www.ticketone.it)
Ticket Web (☎ 02 760 09 131; www.ticketweb.it)

PERFORMING ARTS

Auditorium di Milano
(2, C6)

Abandoned after WWII, the Cinema Massimo was completely reinvented in 1999 through the generosity of an anonymous Milanese donor. It was transformed into the state-of-the-art home to Milan's legendary Giuseppe Verde Symphonic Orchestra, as well as a venue for visiting international jazz acts and chamber music group performances on Sundays.

☎ 02 833 89 201 🖳 www.auditoriumdimilano.org ✉ Largo Gustav Mahler, Corso San Gottardo 42a ❤ box office 10am-7pm Ⓜ Porta Genova

Piccolo Teatro (Teatro Grassi) (3, B4)

This risk-taking little repertory theatre was opened in 1947 by Paolo Grassi and the late, great theatre director Giorgio Strehler and started a massive nationwide movement with avant-garde productions and Commedia dell'Arte revivals. If you are interested in additional programming, including ballet and the Mediterranean Theatre Festival, check out Nuovo Piccolo/Teatro Strehler on Via Rovello 2.

☎ 02 723 33 222 🖳 www.piccoloteatro.org ✉ Via Rovello 2 ❤ box office 10am-6.45pm Mon-Sat Ⓜ Cordusio

CINEMAS

Anteospazio Cinema
(2, C2)

On rainy Mondays in Milan head to Anteospazio, where you can take your pick of three screens showing a range of films, from classics to independents. To fill in time before your show begins, loiter in the bookshop, restaurant and exhibition space. If you are not a fan of dubbing, then you are in luck because Mondays are original-language film days.

☎ 02 659 7732 🖳 www.anteospaziocinema.com ✉ Via Milazzo 9 ❤ open daily Ⓜ Moscova

Cineteca Spazio Oberdan
(2, E3)

The ultimate art-house theatre, showing several screenings daily from its archive of 15,000 films, plus special screenings of films in their original languages as well as seminars with directors.

☎ 02 774 06 300 ✉ Viale Vittorio Veneto 2 ❤ 4-11pm Wed-Sun Ⓜ Porta Venezia

Museo del Cinema (2, D3)

The best way to pick up Italian is to attend screenings of Italian films shown here at 4pm and 5pm, ranging from rare documentary footage of Milanese glitter-rock bands in the 1970s to Sergio Leone's ever-popular Spaghetti Westerns.

☎ 02 655 49 77 ✉ Via Daniele Manin 2 🖳 www.cinetecamilano.it € €3 ❤ 3-6pm Fri-Sun Ⓜ Turati

Ground-breaking theatre at Piccolo Teatro

Sleeping

You're heading to Milan for the sights and shopping, right? Good, because great value is hard to come by in Milanese hotels, with stars assigned as randomly as the Hollywood Walk of Fame. Many charge for amenities you'd take for granted elsewhere, especially at these prices – internet access, breakfast, coffee and tea may be added to your final bill, so ask before you order. That said, there are memorable places to stay in Milan in every price range – just be sure to comparison-shop online for special offers.

DELUXE

Bulgari (3, C2)

From its manicured botanical gardens to black-and-white tuxedo marble bathrooms, the Bulgari is a formal affair. The white minimalist façade is as perfectly aligned as a movie-star smile, and the emerald green spa is paved with gold mosaics more awesome than Oz. Designer Antonio Citterio of B&B Italia fame furnished tropical wood beds with cloud-like coverlets, and meditation corners instead of mere lamps for illumination. ☎ 02 805 80 51 ⬛ www .bulgarihotels.com ✉ Via Privata Fratelli Gabba 7/b Ⓜ Montenapoleone Ⓟ ♿ good 🔀 ✖

Four Seasons Hotel (3, E2)

The nuns who once lived within these cloistered walls wouldn't recognise the place, tricked out in Fortuny fabrics, custom pear-wood furnishings, and Frette linens. Honeymooners will swoon over the garden views and vaulted ceilings in the bi-level suite, and if you can't clinch a business deal in the winsome wood-panelled Visconti suite, rest assured no-one can. ☎ 02 7 70 88 ⬛ www .fourseasons.com/milan ✉ Via Gesù 6/8 Ⓜ Montenapoleone Ⓟ ♿ limited 🔀 ✖ Il Teatro (p52) ♿

Park Hyatt Milano (3, C4)

Designer Ed Tuttle has dressed the Hyatt to impress in sleek Travertine marble and buttery leather. It vaguely resembles the nearby 1930s Palazzo dell'Arengamo – but the Hyatt is too fabulous to be Fascist, with mirrored bathrooms rentable as one-bedrooms in Milan, an in-house spa, diplomatically indirect lighting, and a

Lounge in luxury at the Four Seasons

seamless glass dome easily rising above architectural precedent and relentless neighbourhood construction.
☎ 02 882 11 234 🖥 www .milan.park.hyatt.com
✉ Via Tommaso Grossi 1
Ⓜ Duomo Ⓟ ♿ good
✗ ✗ ✗ ⚥

3Rooms (2, C2)
Apparently, you can sleep in a designer showroom without getting arrested. That's not algae in Room 1's bathroom, it's Bisazza mosaic, and yes, that's an Eames bedspread. Room 2 boasts VIP seating, with a Saarinen leather bum-hugger and Noguchi sofa resembling stacked salami. Room 3 delivers Op-era opulence, with red Arne Jacobsen swan chairs perched upon a swirly black-and-white Vernon Panton rug.
☎ 02 62 61 63
🖥 www.3rooms-10Corso como.com ✉ Corso Como 10 Ⓜ Garibaldi FS
Ⓟ ✗ ✗

TOP END

Grand Hotel et de Milan (3, D2)

Many hotels make grand claims in Milan, but this one's delivered since 1863. Enjoy a post-opera dinner at Don Carlos (p51) before heading up to your spotless antique-appointed room, just as Verdi, Caruso, and Callas have, and you'll be singing in the shower tomorrow. Some ceilings need patching, and single beds shoved together make awkward doubles – otherwise, hospitality is faultless here.
☎ 02 72 31 41 🖥 www .grandhoteletdemilan.it
✉ Via Alessandro Manzoni 29 Ⓜ Montenapoleone
Ⓟ ♿ fair ✗ ✗ ⚥

Hotel Spadari al Duomo (3, B5)

The tranquil blue and gold tones echo Santa Maria presso San Satiro up the street, only the Spadari's comfier, spiffed up with contemporary art, and soundproofed to muffle church bells. Standards here are anything but, and the suites are sweet indeed: snag the garden split-level with the upstairs Jacuzzi, or the terraced suite with the tub overlooking the city.
☎ 02 720 02 371 🖥 www .spadarihotel.com ✉ Via Spadari 11 Ⓜ Duomo
Ⓟ ✗ ✗ ⚥

Hotel Straf (3, D4)

Fashionistas flock here for small, minimalist rooms, high-speed internet and LCD TVs and chroma- and aroma-therapy – never mind that the black lacquer surfaces are cracking, and the polished concrete look is a tad shopworn. Like a model with a chipped tooth, the Straf still stands out in a crowd, even next to the glorious Duomo.
☎ 02 80 50 81 🖥 www .straf.it ✉ Via San Raffaele 3 Ⓜ Duomo
Ⓟ ♿ limited ✗ ✗

JUST YOUR STYLE

Whatever your taste in accommodation, Milan can match it:

Classic Swanky The Four Seasons (opposite), Grand Hotel et de Milan (above) and Antica Locanda Solferino (p70) have all the trappings of luxury, including obligatory etchings, throne-like armchairs and drapes enormous enough to hide a chorus line.

Fashion Forward What you'd expect from Milan is exactly what you'll get at the Bulgari (opposite), 3Rooms (above), Hotel Straf (above) and Enterprise Hotel (p71), all sleek surfaces and cutting edges.

Now & Zen The serenely contemporary Townhouse 31 (p70), Hotel Spadari al Duomo (above), Alle Meravigle (p70) and Park Hyatt (opposite) bid you come in, relax and stay awhile.

Retro Cool Behind their stark modern façades, the Anderson (p70), Mediolanum (p72) and Piccolo (p72) hotels are working a swinging '70s vibe, with bubble light fixtures, teak panelling and low-slung, come-hither couches.

Shop 'Til You Drop If you'd rather spend your cash on shoes than space, the Nuovo (p72), Del Sole (p72), Speronari (p72), Ariosto (p71) and Berna (p70) are bargain-priced near shopping strips.

The ultracool lobby of Hotel Straf (p69)

Townhouse 31 (2, E4)

The espresso and eggnog décor here is sure to leave you relaxed, and possibly thirsty – drinks are served by charming staff outdoors, under a runway tent. African carved wood and decorative eggs add chic ambience, there's wi-fi to ease email withdrawal pangs and piles of pillows guarantee comfort in relatively close quarters. Don't be put off by the pleasant 15-minute walk from Quadrilatero d'Oro, or the price: www.slh.com offers deals.

☎ 02 70 156 🖳 www .townhouse.it ✉ Via Carlo Goldoni 31 Ⓜ Palestro Ⓟ ⊠

MIDRANGE

Alle Meraviglie (3, B3)

Stylists scour Milan for the look Meravigle has mastered: unique, but not overdone. With fresh flowers and wi-fi, offbeat art and no TV, each of the eight rooms is refreshingly distinctive. 'Classic' means small here, so upgrade to a master if you need personal space; make like a model and skip the pricey breakfast.

☎ 02 805 10 23 🖳 www .allemeraviglie.it ✉ Via San Tomaso 8 Ⓜ Cordusio Ⓟ ⊠

Anderson (2, E2)

This sunglass-tinted tower across from the central station is an updated '70s bachelor pad, complete with sunken lobby, mood lighting, wi-fi, red plush rugs and glossy black walls. The wood-panelled rooms are small but stylish, and some bathrooms have flatscreen TVs so you won't miss a second of your AC Milano match, or whatever you're watching on pay-per-view (ahem).

☎ 02 669 01 41 🖳 www .starhotels.it ✉ Piazza Luigi di Savoia 20 Ⓜ Stazione Centrale Ⓟ ♿ fair ⊠ ✕ ⚥

Antica Locanda Solferino (2, C3)

Even though you're ideally located here, no-one would blame you for spooning in your room all day. With period details, bathtubs, wi-fi, lending libraries and satellite TV, these 11 rooms are quaint and cosy. Enjoy your breakfast in bed (usually included with the rate); the hotel has no public areas. Four additional '60s-style apartments have less old-world character, but bonus amenities like Jacuzzis.

☎ 02 657 01 29 🖳 www .anticalocandasolferino.it ✉ Via Castelfidardo 2 Ⓜ Moscova Ⓟ ⊠ ⚥

Berna Hotel (2, E2)

Charming quirks distinguish the Berna: free minibar and internet; vast breakfast buffets including lollipops; and fraternal twin locations, in a mod two-tone building and a turquoise glass tower apparently held together with screws. Rooms are small, as are TVs and the skirts worn by ladies working the block – but kindly staff keeps guests coming back.

☎ 02 67 73 11 🖳 www .hotelberna.com ✉ Via Napo Torriani 18 Ⓜ Stazione Centrale Ⓟ ✕ ⊠ ⚥

TIMING IS EVERYTHING

Fair warning: rates double for rooms you'd be lucky to book six months in advance for the annual **Salone Internazionale del Mobile** (or International Furniture Fair, usually held the third week of April) and **Fashion Week** in autumn (last week of September) or summer (last week of June). Rates for weekends are sometimes 30% to 40% less than weekdays – but late sleepers should bring earplugs, because sound travels in Milanese streets and courtyards.

ROOMS WITH A VIEW

Bulgari (p68) Blooming botanical gardens are a sight for city-sore eyes.

Grand Hotel et de Milan (p69) Milan's best runway show is right below your balcony, along Via Manzoni.

Hotel Speronari (p72) A close-up view of the best backside in Milan: Santa Maria presso San Satiro's.

Park Hyatt (p68) That suite overlooking the Duomo might actually be worth a month's rent.

Enterprise Hotel (2, A2)

Seems like every design mogul has the same Milan agenda: work at the Fiera, play in Sempione, and stay at the Enterprise. You'll be taking taxis or trams downtown, but also enjoying mini-spa bathrooms, filling buffet breakfasts, plush bathrobes and slippers. A suite here basically means a bigger desk, so stick with leather-clad, parquet-floored standard rooms with wi-fi and splurge on shoes at nearby Mercato Fauché.

☎ 02 3 18 18 🖵 www
.enterprisehotel.com
✉ Corso Sempione 91
Ⓜ Lotto 🚊 1,14,19,33
🅿 ♿ fair ⛶ ✗

Gran Duca di York (3, B5)

At last, a historic hotel with beds far more comfy than your grandma's, where you won't bark your shins on clunky antiques. All 33 tasteful yellow-striped rooms were updated in 2004, though the soundproofing isn't perfect – but at these prices, this close to the Duomo, you can spring for earplugs. Breakfast is free and tasty, with fresh fruit and copious cold cuts.

☎ 02 87 48 63 🖵 www
.ducadiyork.com ✉ Via Moneta 1 Ⓜ Duomo 🅿 ⛶ ✗

Hotel Ariosto (2, B3)

Outside, the Ariosto has the architectural charms of its Art Nouveau neighbours, but inside it's more forward-thinking, offering free internet and bicycles, air con, Jacuzzis and power showers – plus some unfortunate sponge-painted wall treatments. You may've come for *Il Cenacolo* nearby, but don't skip the free breakfast; the Ariosto offers quite a spread.

☎ 02 481 78 44 🖵 www
.brerahotels.com ✉ Via Ludvico Ariosto 22 Ⓜ Conciliazione 🅿 ✗ ⛶

Hotel Ariston (3, A6)

Conveniently located à couple of blocks from both Corso Porta Ticinese and Brera boutiques, the Ariston's perfect for ecologically minded shoppers, with organic breakfasts, chemical-free paint and pleasantly spare, snug rooms kept spotless with nontoxic cleaners. Free bicycles are available for guests more concerned about emissions than personal safety.

☎ 02 720 00 556 🖵 www
.brerahotels.com ✉ Largo Carrobbio 2 Ⓜ Sant'
Ambrogio 🅿 ✗ ⛶

Breathe freely at Hotel Ariston, where there are no toxic nasties

Hotel Mediolanum (2, E2)
Behind that severe exterior is a sly sense of humour, with pop-art paint jobs and original 1970s furnishings delivering snappy comebacks. Too bad those giant radio dials don't work, and the white goose-neck lamps are on the blink – but the bathrooms are immaculate, wi-fi is available and colourful toiletries a treat. Disregard the laughable official rates; bargains are available online.
☎ 02 670 53 12 🖳 www .mediolanumhotel.com ✉ Via Mauro Macchi 1 Ⓜ Stazione Centrale Ⓟ ✂ ✣

BUDGET

Hotel Del Sole (2, E2)
Stay in these pleasant, spacious rooms a few days, and the friendly staff starts treating you like a relative – only you're not expected to make your own bed. The two rooms with lovely private terraces are as coveted as sample-sale Prada; book yours now.
☎ 02 295 12 971 🖳 www.delsolehotel.com

✉ Via Gaspare Spontini 6 Ⓜ Lima ✣

Hotel Speronari (3, C5)
Want your Italian room with a view for under €100? Forget Florence and head to the Speronari, where you can throw open your shutters and marvel at Bramante's Santa Maria presso San Satiro. Gloomy hallways lead to spacious, clean, high-ceilinged rooms with clean private or shared bathrooms.
☎ 02 864 61 125; fax 02 720 03178 ✉ Via Speronari 4 Ⓜ Duomo

Il Postello (2, C1)
Ten euro lets you bunk in with artists, activists and anarchists in this community centre at the heart of Milan's underground scene. The kitchen serves tasty organic vegetarian fare and bike rental is free; no wonder stays are limited to 10 days. Staff don't always answer phone calls or email when they're busy booking bands for Saturday night in the garden – keep trying.
☎ 02 333 175 22 72 🖳 http://postello.reality

hacking.org ✉ Via della Pergola 5 Ⓜ Garibaldi FS

Nuovo Hotel (3, E5)
Five-star hotels must envy the Nuovo's location, in a quiet pedestrian street right behind the Duomo. Only one floor has air conditioning, but the spare, spotless rooms have TVs and decent-sized private or shared bathrooms, and the gruff desk staff turn into teddy bears once you try out your Italian.
☎ 02 864 64 444 🖳 www .hotelnuovomilano.com ✉ Piazza Beccaria 6 Ⓜ Duomo ✣

Piccolo Hotel (2, A2)
Like the perfect vintage shirt, this funky hotel is a real find in mint condition. With a circular front desk, swivel lamps, bucket chairs, and wood panelling, you'll think you've entered a groovy '70s film set. The sights are a taxi or tram ride away, but great clubs are nearby.
☎ 02 336 01 775 🖳 www .piccolohotelmilano.it ✉ Via Piero della Francesca 60 Ⓜ Lotto 🚋 1,14,19,33 Ⓟ

Set up home for a few days in the spacious rooms at Hotel Del Sole

About Milan

HISTORY
Romans, Rebels & One Hairy Boar

Contrary to opinions cultivated over the past two-and-a-half millennia, Milan was founded not by well-heeled urbanites, but meandering Insubri Celts. According to legend, this settlement site was chosen when the king glimpsed a bristle-backed boar on the horizon – visions of Milanese salami, perhaps? The Insubri considered invading Rome, but the Romans beat them to the punch in 222 BC. Milan became a Roman armaments manufacturing centre, but the Milanese chafed under Roman authority; a popular insurrection in AD 385 signalled the decline of Roman control.

Not-So-Friendly Competition

Attila the Hun's crew and various Goths had their way with the city before the Germanic Lombards took over in 569. Lombard Queen Theodolinda officially converted her queendom from Arianism to Christianity, but common religion didn't resolve Lombard feuds with the Franks. Charlemagne claimed Milan for the Holy Roman Empire in 774, but the archdiocese's attempt to take control resulted in struggles to the death between would-be masters of Milan and its not-about-to-be vassals.

Milan finally found peace in the 11th century, forming an ambitious *comune* (town council) that began building commercial canals. Cremona, Mantua, and Bergamo didn't appreciate the competition, and Holy Roman Emperor Frederick Barbarossa exploited local rivalries to overthrow Milan in 1162. Milan put up an 11-month fight and furious Frederick razed the city upon its surrender. This seemed a tad excessive to neighbouring towns, who formed the Lega Lombarda with Milan, and kicked Frederick to the curb in 1176.

Empires & Epidemics

The arts flourished under the Visconti dynasty, who attracted Italy's best artisans and began the Duomo in 1386. Gian Galeazzo Visconti donated the rosy-grey Candoglia marble, transported to Milan via canals – unfortunately, plague-infested rats came along for the ride.

Soon 30,000 Milanese had died, and the rest mostly starved

Medieval Porta Ticinese – gateway to style

Feathered frenzy at Piazza del Duomo

until the city stabilised under Ludovico Sforza in the 1480s. His brilliant wife Beatrice d'Este is widely credited with bringing da Vinci and Bramante to Milan, and proved an effective ambassador for the Sforzas – all before dying in childbirth at age 22. The French usurped power from the Sforzas in 1499, but they were no match for microbes: between 1524 and 1528 another epidemic wiped out 80,000 people and the weakened city fell under Spanish rule in 1535.

Spanish Milan was literally plagued with problems. In 1576, 17,000 Milanese died of plague, and the 1629–30 plague killed 7000 more. Paranoia swept the city, and terminally ill plague victims were accused of purposely dabbing their germs on public monuments – a fictitious crime somewhat redundantly punishable by death. With more trouble than tax revenues to offer, Milan was handed to the Austrians in 1713. The city rose again under Austrian Empress Maria Theresa, and the facades of La Scala and the Palazzo Reale remain her favourite shade of yellow.

All That Glitters

Perhaps Maria Theresa should have chosen a less eye-catching colour, because her nemesis Napoleon never could resist the glint of gold. He claimed Milan in 1805, crowning himself king of Italy in the Duomo. Austria regained control from 1814 to 1859, until troops commandeered by Vittorio Emanuele II and Napoleon III defeated the Austrians at the Battle of Magenta. Milan celebrated joining the Kingdom of Italy in 1860 with a binge on opulent architecture, from the morbidly glamorous Cimitero Monumentale to the Galleria Vittorio Emanuele II shopping paradise.

But not everyone was enjoying the high life in Milan and workers drove this point home with some of Europe's first mass strikes in 1872. Another strike in 1898 was brutally crushed; 83 people were killed in just four days. To track dramatic events as they unfolded, Milan's staunchly independent *Corriere della Sera* was founded in 1876, and landmark leftist *Critica Sociale* in 1891.

Life During Wartime

Milan hadn't yet recovered from its losses from WWI when influenza struck in 1918. Six thousand people died and the city plunged into economic depression. Mussolini's promise to restore Italy's strength appealed to many in 1922, when the Fascists rose to power. San Siro stadium was inaugurated in 1926, symbolising Fascism's promise to bring back the glory days of ancient Rome – but with unstable foundations of intolerance and absolutism, Fascism was destined to fall harder and faster than the Roman Empire.

Petrified Emperor Constantine gazes down upon modern Milan

During WWII, bombardment by the Allied forces demolished about a quarter of Milan, leaving La Scala and much of the centre in ruins. When Milanese factory workers risked prison to protest Fascist rule in 1943, Mussolini's legitimacy was undermined. Italy surrendered to Allied forces on 8 September 1943, but two weeks later Mussolini declared a new Fascist republic in Salò, forcing a long, bloody fight against the Allies and fellow Italians.

The Italian Resistance prevailed in 1945, when a three-day Milanese insurrection ended Nazi occupation, and Mussolini was shot dead. But for Milanese who'd been bombed while Mussolini grandstanded, that wasn't enough. The corpses of Mussolini and his mistress were hung upside down from a petrol station on Piazzale Loreto, and pelted with stones.

COMING CLEAN

In 1992 Milan initiated the *Mani Pulite* (Clean Hands) investigation into corruption – and it's not done yet. Native son Silvio Berlusconi was implicated in bribery scandals and despite a self-granted immunity to prosecution, the taint hastened his ouster as prime minister in 2006. Recently the *Calciopoli* game-rigging scandal resulted in unprecedented penalties against five Series A football clubs, including AC Milan. Its director? One Silvio Berlusconi. The latest is *Valettopoli*, where intercepted mobile phone calls reveal *valette*, TV spokesmodels, were being passed around by Italian entertainment moguls like party favours. Who controls 90% of Italy's TV conglomerates? That's right, the Berlusconi family, but perhaps not for long – Italy and the EU are now challenging Berlusconi's consolidation of Italian media in the courts.

THE WRITING ON THE WALL

Some call it art, others call it vandalism – but in Milan, graffiti is inescapable. Historically, graffiti has been a consistent outlet for protest throughout Milan's many eras of occupation and repressive rule, when petitions and marches weren't exactly options. Today, football team slogans and declarations of undying love compete for wall space with political refrains like *'Piu case, meno chiese'* (More houses, less churches) and *'no a Bush, no alla guerra'* (no to Bush, no to war). Sometimes entire structures are covered with commentary, such as Pergola Move, inside **Il Postello** (p72) and the famous 'Graffiti Bridge' over the metro tracks from Porta Genova to Via Tortona. This footbridge also provides a close-up view of subway cars 'bombed' with Milan's baroque take on New York's wild-style graffiti, parked alongside trains covered in wrap-around advertisements – in Milan, art, commerce, and anarchy are never far apart.

Comebacks & Kickbacks

The post-war car manufacturing boom produced yet another of Milan's trademark growth spurts. Italy's first student movement kicked off in Milan in 1968, bringing dissent, free love, and psychedelic fashions to the fore. But life in Milan was not all fast cars, fast women, protests and Pucci galore. Growing income gaps and mass migration from southern Italy inflamed underlying social tensions. In the 1970s, Brigade Rosse terrorism and repressive anti-terror laws created further turmoil, and gave rise to extremist groups like Lega Nord.

The prosperous '80s and '90s brought some stability to Milan – or so it seemed. Corruption and organised crime malingered behind closed doors until the *Tangentopoli* (Bribesville) scandals broke in 1992 (see boxed text p75). The next shocker was the 1995 Mafia-hit murder of fashion mogul Maurizio Gucci ordered by his estranged wife, followed by a rash of mob hits in 1999. But with a vigilant judiciary and local press, Milan seems to be learning from past oversights. History isn't a footnote in Milan; it's a work in progress.

Take your pick from postcards capturing the many faces of Milanese splendour

ENVIRONMENT

Industry has taken its toll on Milan's environment, but in recent years Milan has started reclaiming industrial 'brown sites' and turned them into green spaces. Recycling has become a household religion here, with multiple recycling bins in every courtyard.

Air quality is another story, and not a happy one. A malevolent haze often hovers over the city, the result of comparatively lax industry regulation and traffic emissions. With spiralling petrol prices and byways in the centre becoming pedestrian streets, the metro and shoe leather seem like ever more essential transport options.

GOVERNMENT & POLITICS

After years of leaning right with business interests, Milan is swinging leftward with the rest of Italy. In 2006, right-wing prime minister Silvio Berlusconi was narrowly ousted by centrist challenger Romano Prodi. Milan's mayoral race was also close, obliging new centre-right mayor Letizia Moratti to court the left to form a coalition government – no easy feat. Milan has a reputation for extremes as the birthplace of both Italy's anarchist movement and ultraright Lega Nord, and home to Berlusconi and Dario Fo, the Nobel Prize–winning playwright whose 2006 Communist Party mayoral bid rallied Milan's left.

Most Milanese are as vocal about local politics as they are about football – though for many, both are spectator sports. Many locals aren't eligible to vote here, including foreign residents and the growing numbers of Milan's workforce that live in bedroom communities outside the city. So while political concerns are often aired over aperitivi, they aren't always reflected in the city's polls.

ECONOMY

The city that brushed off the ashes of war to become a captain of industry has shaken the soot of heavy manufacturing off its well-tailored shoulders. Milan has become Italy's centre for publishing, TV, music, advertising, high-tech, financial services, and design, earning some 20% of Italy's gross domestic product.

But while business is booming for Europe's fifth-largest urban economy, many Milanese are still staggering from inflation following Italy's 2002 conversion to the euro. Resourceful Milanese have adapted as stylishly as possible, making dinners of aperitivi, mobbing free art gallery openings, and (gasp) buying last season's shoes on sale. Travellers who do likewise will enjoy good company with all the pizzazz and none of the pretension of the *fighetti*, the widely derided fashion victims of Milan's industrialist caste.

DID YOU KNOW?
- Almost 50 million pounds of cheese are produced annually in Lombardy.
- Lombardy accounts for 30% of Italy's exports.
- 94% of Milan's businesses have less than 10 employees, and 25% of Milan's workforce is freelance.
- 320,000 people pass through Milan's Stazione Centrale every day.

Milan's hip bar culture continues to thrive

SOCIETY & CULTURE

Casually cosmopolitan Milan has had more experience with immigration than most other European cities, and it shows. Migration to Milan began almost right after WWII and soon transformed the broken, battered city into the economic miracle of southern Europe. In moments of amnesiac ingratitude, some Milanese may grouse about *immigrati* (immigrants) or refer to people from southern Italy as *terrone*, a derogatory term meaning 'people of the earth.' However overall, Milanese are quite pragmatically accepting of foreigners –and even other Italians – in their midst (below).

Today the city has about 1.3 million people, but add the bedroom communities that border it and supply its workforce, and that number swells to over 2.5 million. Fewer Milanese live in the centre of the city than ever before, so many of the city's best restaurants and clubs now dot the peripheries, closer to where most Milanese spend their downtime.

MILAN'S MONDO PICCOLO

To hear many Milanese boast about the 'international character' of their city, you'd think diversity was a dish they'd invented, like saffron risotto. Though foreign residents represent only 2% of the population, their contributions to Milan's cultural life are anything but minor. Anyone who can cook, photograph, kick or drive like a maniac fits right in, so creative types, models, footballers, and race car drivers are all automatic Milanese. In this *mondo piccolo* (small world), Eritreans are neighbours to Lebanese and Latin Americans north of Corso Buenos Aires, in an area packed with galleries and restaurants jokingly referred to as 'the Kasbah'. Milan's Chinese community has settled into Via Sarpi, where winebars offering fusion aperitivi compete for prime stomach real estate with 'Chinese sushi' – and why not? This is Milan, where Sri Lankans, Italians, and Slovenians banter and bargain multilingually at the Mercato Papiniano (p50). The Milanese may not have invented diversity, but they pull it off with a certain panache.

Etiquette

Many visitors are awed by sophisticated Milanese, and their knack of speaking with great assurance about any subject – including things they know nothing about. But the secret to social life in Milan is that no-one expects their opinions to be politely accepted; every opinion invites another. Contradictions are opportunities for friendly banter, while agreement is often expressed with the vehemence of an argument: 'No, Paul Smith is not an innovative menswear designer – he is *the* innovative menswear designer!'

Not long into such an animated conversation, you may find yourself agreeing to go along to a show, café or restaurant with people you've only just met. Once the ice is broken, Milanese will go out of their way to show you a good time. But if you make an appointment, don't be late; punctuality is a sign of respect here.

ARTS

Music

For at least two centuries, Milan has been home to some of the world's foremost musicians, most demanding conductors, and toughest audiences – the Verdi Home for Retired Musicians is the only place in town musicians are allowed some slack. The electric air of expectation fills Milan's music venues with collective adrenaline, pushing musicians to perform even when the house is half-empty. Concerts begin with audiences already on the edge of their seats, knowing that the musicians risk derision if they fail to reach new heights; but when they succeed, the euphoria of the crowd is like none other.

La Scala and the Giuseppe Verdi Orchestra aren't the only shows in town. Home to more than 20 independent labels and Italy's major music publishers, Milan is also famous for jazz and an alternative scene featuring fun, suspiciously well-groomed pop-punk bands. Like any city in Italy, you'll fill up fast on pernicious pop ballads, generic dance, and bland hip-hop. But don't let that spoil your appetite for the Milan Jazz Festival, and the pogo-until-you-pull-a-muscle Rock in Idro.

Fashion

Milan started turning heads after WWII, when Italy's fashion industry outgrew Florence. Then Milanese designers Rosita and Ottavio Missoni unveiled more than their signature knitwear at a 1967 runway show, where the combination of gossamer fabrics, braless models, and strong lights caused one of the fashion world's

Milan's fashion future shines so bright

first scandals. Among the fashion hopefuls making the scene in '70s Milan were Krizia, Giorgio Armani and Gianni Versace. It's hard to picture the '80s without such Milan fashion staples as Gucci belts and Benetton sweaters, or the '90s without double-stick-taped dresses by Dolce & Gabbana and Roberto Cavalli. Milanese Miuccia Prada built her fashion empire from the ground up, starting with shoes ideal for romantic dates in outer space; La Perla went with the inside-out approach, creating unmentionables worth mentioning. Even if you've seen London, France and enough underpants, Milan's twice-annual Fashion Week is certain to raise eyebrows, and lower bank reserves.

Architecture & Design

Walking down a Milan sidewalk is like playing hopscotch through the centuries. The early Renaissance is just a hop, skip and a jump from avant-garde by way of gothic, rococo, futurism, Fascism, post-war functionalism, '60s mod, '70s funk and postmodernism – not necessarily in that order. War left gaping holes in the cityscape that were filled in fast by Milan's reigning powers and booming industries – too fast, some would say with a glance at the neo-Soviet buildings lining Via Vittor Pisani.

But the lack of consistency in Milan's architecture brings a bonanza of eclecticism. The glass sails of Massimiliano Fuksas' experimental Fiera seem to get their momentum from the soaring gothic Duomo, Castello Sforsezco mixes and matches Bramante, da Vinci and 19th century masonry by Luca Beltrami, and Mario Botta's round rear addition to La Scala almost makes sense. The lack of a dominant Milanese aesthetic has freed local and international architects to get inventive. New landmarks by the likes of Zaha Hadid, Arata Isozaki, and Daniel Libeskind are in the works, and Milan's Salone Internazionale del Mobile (International Furniture Fair) represents the world's best guesses about homes of the future.

The versatile Palazzo Reale – from medieval town hall to gallery extraordinaire (p27)

Visual Arts

Elegant arbours adorn Art Nouveau façades

Museums in Milan are jewel boxes containing priceless works of art from the Renaissance to the rococo, including signature works by Leonardo da Vinci, Giovanni Bellini, Andrea Mantegna, Bernardino Luini, Caravaggio, and Tintoretto. But the city also holds a wealth of futurist paintings by Umberto Boccioni and Giacomo Balla that still seem shockingly new, especially when seen in the neoclassical context of the Museo dell'Ottocento. Many of Italy's favourite 19th- and 20th-century masterpieces can be found here: Francesco Hayez' eternally Romantic *The Kiss,* as well as Giuseppe da Volpedo's *Fourth Estate*, with pointillist workers making impressionism look radical in pink. Aesthetic rebel Lucio Fontana's 1950s slash paintings at the Museo di Boschi di San Stefano literally poked holes in the concept of painting as something separate from sculpture. Milan's contemporary art galleries (p23) take it from there, daring you to find pieces that viewers will still be admiring (or wondering about) years from now.

Performing Arts

Milan without theatre and dance seems unthinkable, but after two wars, its future in the theatre was hardly certain. Instead of staging a grand comeback, Milan decided to start small in 1947 with the Piccolo Teatro (Little Theatre), which featured cheap ticket prices and promoted risk-taking productions. The Piccolo Teatro staged Dario Fo's 1971 triumph *Accidental Death of an Anarchist*, and just last year overcame controversy to stage Fo's latest work: *The Two-Headed Anomaly*, a satirical production about Berlusconi and his wife. The Piccolo proved too popular for its size, leading to other less *piccolo* Piccolo Teatros throughout Milan as well as across the country. Today theatre-goers in Milan are spoiled for choice with 25 major theatres and many smaller ones opening with the regularity of a Milanese theatre buff's pocketbook.

Brush up on your Italian at the movies

Directory

ARRIVAL & DEPARTURE
Air

Most intra-Europe and international flights use **Malpensa airport** (4, A2), 50km northwest of the city. Most domestic flights use **Linate airport** (4,B3), 7km east of the city centre, and a few low-cost European airlines use **Orio al Serio airport** (4, C2).

MALPENSA AIRPORT
Information 🖥 www.sea-aeroporti milano.it
Flight Information ☎ 02 748 52 200
Lost Property Office ☎ 02 748 62 900

Airport Access

A taxi from Malpensa to downtown Milan costs about €75 and takes 50 minutes or longer, depending on traffic.

The **Malpensa Express** (☎ 02 202 22; 🖥 www.malpensaexpress.it; 📅 ticket office 6.30am-9.50pm Mon-Sun) connects Malpensa airport to **Stazione Nord/Cadorna** (📅 ticket office 6am-8.20pm Mon-Sun), or vice versa, in 40 minutes; trains leave every 30 minutes between 6am and 10pm. One-way tickets cost €11/5.50 at the ticket office, or €2.50 more on the train. Malpensa Express runs a late-night/early-morning bus service that takes 50 minutes; pick-up/drop-off is on Via Paleocapa at Stazione Nord.

The **Malpensa Shuttle coach service** (☎ 02 585 83 185; 🖥 www.malpensa-shuttle.com; 📅 ticket office 7am-9pm; €5/2.50) runs between Malpensa and Stazione Centrale every 20 minutes from 5am to 10.30pm, and takes about 50 minutes.

Pick-up/drop-off is at Piazza Luigi di Savoia, outside Stazione Centrale.

LINATE AIRPORT
Information 🖥 www.sea-aeroporti milano.it
Flight Information ☎ 02 748 52 200
Airport Access
Taxis to/from Linate airport to downtown Milan cost €15 to €18. Alternatively, the **Starfly bus** (☎ 02 585 87 23; €3) runs to/from Stazione Centrale every 30 minutes from about 6am to midnight and takes about 30 minutes. Pick-up/drop-off is at Piazza Luigi di Savoia, near Stazione Centrale. **ATM bus 73** (from cnr of Corso Europa; one-way €1) runs to/from central Piazza San Babila every 10 minutes from 6am to 12.55am, and takes about 20 minutes. ATM tickets must be bought in advance at newsstands or tobacconists.

ORIO AL SERIO AIRPORT
Information 🖥 www.orioaeroporto.it
Flight Information ☎ 03 532 63 23
Lost & Found ☎ 03 532 62 97

Airport Access
Autostradale buses (☎ 03 531 84 72; 🖥 www.autostradale.it; one-way €6.90 /3.45) run to/from Stazione Centrale every 30 to 45 minutes between 4.30am and 1am, and take about an hour. The **Orio Shuttle** (☎ 03 531 93 66; 🖥 www .orioshuttle.com; €6/3) runs nonstop to/from Stazione Centrale about every 50 minutes between 4am and midnight, and takes 65 minutes.

CLIMATE CHANGE & TRAVEL
Travel – especially air travel – is a significant contributor to global climate change. At Lonely Planet, we believe that all travellers have a responsibility to limit their personal impact. As a result, we have teamed with Rough Guides and other concerned industry partners to support Climatecare.org, which allows travellers to offset the greenhouse gases they are responsible for with contributions to sustainable travel schemes. Lonely Planet offsets all staff and author travel. For more information, check out www.lonelyplanet.com/climatecare.

Bus

Long-distance buses depart from **Garibaldi bus station** (☎ 02 63 79 01; Piazza Sigmund Freud).

Train

Trains to cities throughout Italy and Europe leave from **Stazione Centrale** (2, E1; Piazza Duca d'Aosta; station information office; ☎ 147 88 8088; ☺ 7am-9pm). Tickets can be purchased online through Trenitalia (🖳 www.trenitalia.it), or from ticket machines inside the station. Trains to Lombardy destinations leave from **Stazione Nord** (2, B4; ☎ 02 20222; Piazza Luigi Cadorna), and points northwest of Milan are served by **Stazione Porta Garibaldi** (2, C2; ☎ 02 655 20 78; Piazza Sigmund Freud).

Travel Documents
PASSPORT

EU citizens only need a valid passport or national ID card to enter Italy. To get a visa for Italy, your passport must be valid for several months after the date of entry.

VISA

Nationals of Australia, Canada, Japan, New Zealand and the USA don't need a visa for visits up to three months; other nationals should check with their local Italian embassy or consulate. Special visas may be required for students, long-term visitors and anyone taking up employment in Italy.

Customs & Duty Free

Travellers from non-EU countries can import up to 200 cigarettes, 1L of spirits, 2L of wine, 50mL of perfume, and 250mL of eau de toilette duty free.

Left Luggage

Most hotels will hold your luggage at reception short-term without charge (a gratuity is appreciated), or you can leave it here at the following stations:

Stazione Centrale (2, E1; ☎ 02 637 12 667; ☺ 3am-1am)
Stazione Nord (2, B4; ☎ 800 557 730; ☺ 5.15am-11.30pm)
Stazione Porta Garibaldi (2, C2; ☎ 02 655 20 78; €4; ☺ 7am-8.30pm)

GETTING AROUND

The best way to contend with Milanese traffic is **ATM**, Milan's network of buses, trams, and the Metro. Public transport maps are available from ATM's **Info Point** (3, C5; located in Duomo metro station; ☺ 7.45am-8.15pm Mon-Sat; Ⓜ Duomo).

Travel Passes

ATM tickets costs €1 and are valid for one Metro ride, or 75 minutes of travel on buses and trams. Books of 10 tickets cost €9.20, unlimited one-day passes cost €3 and two-day passes cost €5.50. Tickets are sold at Metro stations, newsstands, and tobacconists.

Bus & Trams

Buses and trams are usually more efficient than driving through traffic and finding parking in Milan, and they reach points where metro stops are few and far between. Most run between 6am and midnight, with routes clearly marked by yellowish signposts. New digital displays have been installed at some stops, but you would probably have better luck consulting a fortune teller – that sign promising another tram in nine minutes may make the same promise in 20. Validate your ticket by punching it in one of the machines on board – otherwise, you could be fined.

Metro

The **Metro** (☎ 800 808 181; 🖳 www.atm-mi.it) is the best way to travel in Milan, with frequent trains from 6am to midnight on the red MM1, green MM2, and yellow MM3 lines. The blue line on Metro maps is the Passante Ferroviario, a commuter train service to outlying areas.

Bicycle

Only fearless bikers should take on Milan's cobblestones, daredevil drivers and nonexistent bike lanes. To protest the lack of infrastructure for bikes, **Critical Mass** (💻 www.criticalmass.it) bike-parade protests hit the streets the last Friday of every month – some bikers go nude in summer.

To help reduce Milan's traffic emissions, hotels such as Ariston (p71) and Il Postello (p72) offer guests free bicycle use. For bike rentals, go to **AWS Bici Motor** (2, E1; ☎ 02 670 72 145; Via Ponte Seveso 33, cnr Via Schiaparelli). The safest, most enjoyable biking itinerary is around Navigli on weekends. On summer nights, Navigli streets are closed to outside traffic between 8pm and 2am.

Taxi

Taxi stands are located near major piazzas. Though taxis don't often stop when hailed, you may have luck on slow nights. Calling a taxi costs more, as the meter starts when the taxi accepts your order and heads over to pick you up. Dispatchers don't usually speak English, but your hotel concierge can call for you (☎ 02 40 40, 02 69 69 or 02 85 85).

Car & Motorcycle

By not driving in Milan, you'll be doing yourself and Milan's air a favour. Blue lines mark street parking, but when you find a spot, don't get too excited: it's not free and is only limited to two hours. Buy a Sosta Milano card from a tobacconist, scratch off the date and time, then display it in your car. For overnight parking, ask your hotel about nearby garages. Don't park in yellow residents-only spaces or tow-away zones – they're not kidding.

ROAD RULES

There are some road rules in Milan, although you would never know it from the city's traffic jams. Some basics: the city speed limit is usually 50km/hour or under; seat belts are required; children under 12

must travel in the back seat. Most Italian highways are toll roads, and the highway speed limit is 130km/hour to 150km/hour.

RENTAL

Hertz, Avis, Maggiore and Europcar have offices at Stazione Centrale and Malpensa and Linate airports; Orio Al Serio airport has Hertz, Maggiore and Europcar offices. For better parking, rent a scooter, motorcycle, or SMART car at **ADM** (2, C3; ☎ 02 657 00 49; 💻 www.thanks.it/adm; Via della Moscova 47). For scooters or motorcycles, you need a class B motorcycle/scooter licence, and law requires you to wear a helmet.

DRIVING LICENCE & PERMIT

If you're from an EU member state, your current driving licence is valid here; others need an International Driving Permit (IDP). Always carry proof of ownership or rental for the vehicle you're driving, car insurance papers and your passport.

MOTORING ORGANISATIONS

Automobile Club Italia (ACI; 2, D4; ☎ 02 774 51; 💻 www.aci.it; Corso Venezia 43) has reciprocal service arrangements with many EU automobile associations.

PRACTICALITIES
Climate & When to Go

The best months to visit Milan are April, May, June, September and October – but book well ahead during trade fairs and Fashion Weeks. Winter is mostly foggy and rainy, since mountains shield Milan from winter extremes. On sunny days and all of August everyone heads to parks or Navigli.

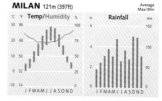

MILAN 121m (397ft)

Consulates
Australia (3, F4; ☎ 02 77 70 41; 🖳 www
.italy.embassy.gov.au; Via Borgogna 2)
Canada (2, D2; ☎ 02 6 75 81; 🖳 www
.canada.it; Via Vittor Pisani 19)
France (2, D3; ☎ 02 655 91 41; 🖳 www
.france-italia.it; Via Cesare Mangile 1)
Germany (2, C3; ☎ 02 623 11 01; Via
Solferino 40)
New Zealand (2, A4; ☎ 02 480 12 544;
🖳 www.mfat.govt.nz; Via Guido
d'Arezzo 6)
UK (3, D4; ☎ 02 723 001; 🖳 www.british
embassy.gov.uk ; Via San Paolo 7
US (2, D3; ☎ 02 290 351; 🖳 http://milan
.usconsulate.gov; Via Principe Amedeo 2/10)

Disabled Travellers
Cobblestone streets without footpaths,
narrow elevators, steps without ramps,
wheelchair-inaccessible toilets and an-
archic traffic are among the accessibility
concerns Italy is beginning to address.
Milan's ATM is making system-wide transport improvements, and **Milano Per Tutti**
(www.milanopertutti.it) offers suggested
itineraries and accessibility information
for major monuments. Accessible venues
are marked in this guide with ♿ .

Discounts
STUDENT & YOUTH CARDS
Full-time students with an **International
Student Identity Card** (ISIC 🖳 www
.isiccard.com) get discounts on admission
fees, services and air fares. Nonstudents
under 26 should get the **Euro<26 Card**
(🖳 www.euro26.org) – look on the website for discounts at 200 Milanese venues,
including bike rentals, beauty salons and
pubs.

Electricity
Voltage 220V
Frequency 50Hz
Cycle AC
Plugs standard continental: two round pins

Emergencies
Ambulance (☎ 118)
Carabinieri military police (☎ 112)
Fire (☎ 115)
Foreigners' Police Office (☎ 02 6 22 61;
Via Montebello 26)
Police (☎ 113 English-speaking operator
02 86 37 01)
Police Station (3, D1; ☎ 02 6 22 61; Via
Fatebenefratelli 11)

Fitness
Big hotels and some wellness centres
have swimming pools, gym facilities
and exercise classes. Otherwise, most
require subscriptions. **Downtown Pal-
estre** (☎ 02 760 14 85; Piazza Cavour
2; ☽ 7am-midnight Mon-Fri, 10am-9pm
Sat-Sun; Ⓜ Turati) has good equipment,
a sizable swimming pool, and a sizable
€60 per day rate.

SWIMMING
Cozzi (2, D2; ☎ 02 659 97 03; Viale
Tunisia 35; ☽ noon-11.30pm Mon,
7.30am-5.30pm Tue & Thu, 8.30am-
10.30pm Wed, 8.30am-9pm Fri, 10am-
5.30pm Sat; closed Aug, limited hours
in winter; Ⓜ Porta Venezia) Centrally
located pool with diving boards.
Lido (☎ 02 392 66 100; Piazzale Lorenzo
Lotto 15; ☽ 10am-7pm Tue-Sat; limited
hours in winter; €4 ; Ⓜ Lotto) Waterslides
and aquatic amusements, plus a
rollerblading rink.
Piscina Solari (2, A5; ☎ 02 469 52 78;
Via Montevideo 11; €4; ☽ 10am-9.20pm
Mon-Fri, Sat 12.30-5pm May-Jul;
closed Aug, limited hours in winter;
Ⓜ Sant'Agostino) Public pool by day;
cocktail venue on summer nights.

Gay & Lesbian Travellers
Milan attracts visitors from around the
country and all over the world with the
promise of good times, good food and of
course great clothes had by all – just as

long as you are wearing your good shoes, no-one in Milan really cares who your date might be. On any given Saturday night, it seems that Milan could be worlds away from the Vatican and its condemnations of homosexuality, though not beyond its influence – due largely to pressure received from the Vatican, Italy has not yet legalised civil unions, as countries like Spain have.

Special gay calendar events like Milan's Gay & Lesbian Film Festival, annual June Pride parade and Gay Open Tennis Championship in September bring the masses to Milan, and so do trend-setting 'gay-friendly' (and straight-friendly) clubs and bars. Your best bets can be found in this book; additional gay-friendly venues can be found at www.gay friendlyitaly.com and www.gay.it/guida. Only at the occasional sex club are new patrons asked to produce a membership card for the Italian gay/les/bi/trans organisation **Arcigay** (2, E5; ☎ 02 541 22 225; ⌨ www.arcigaymilano.org; Via Bezzecca 3) – as a non-Italian, you can obtain entry to almost anywhere without proof of prior gayness.

Health
IMMUNISATIONS
No vaccinations are required to enter Italy.

PRECAUTIONS
Health risks in Milan are mostly sunburn, overindulgence and new-shoes blisters.

MEDICAL SERVICES
Milan Clinic (3, F4; ☎ 02 760 16 047; ⌨ www.milanclinic.com; Via Cerva 25; Ⓜ San Babila) Private clinic with some English-speaking doctors, including dentists, gynaecologists, and optometrists.

Ospedale Maggiore Policlinico (2, D5; ☎ English speakers 02 5 50 31, non-English speakers 02 550 33171; Via Francesco Sforza 35; Ⓜ Crocetta) All European Union citizens have free access to this public hospital, whereas others may have to pay for nonemergency services.

PHARMACIES
For after-hours needs, check out ⌨ www .milanclinic.com/pharmacies.htm or listings of late-night pharmacies in pharmacy windows.
24-hour Pharmacy (2, E2; ☎ 02 669 09 35; Stazione Centrale, upper gallery)
Farmacia Carlo Erba (3, C4; ☎ 02 87 86 68; Piazza del Duomo 21; ⌚ 9pm-8.30am)

Holidays
Public transport may be limited during holidays, and shops and restaurants closed on these days:

New Year's Day	1 January
Epiphany	6 January
Easter Monday	March/April
Liberation Day	25 April
Labour Day	1 May
Feast of the Assumption	15 August
All Saints Day	1 November
Festa di Sant'Ambrogio	7 December
Feast of the Immaculate Conception	8 December
Christmas Day	25 December
Festa di S Stefano	26 December

Internet
INTERNET ACCESS
Most hotels have internet access, though not many wireless access available and service can sometimes be spotty. For more reliable access, use the services listed below.
All Web Business & Arts (3, B5; ☎ 02 454 78 874 ; ⌨ www.allwebusinessarts .it; Via Valpetrosa 5; per hour €3; Ⓜ Duomo)

Internet Enjoy (☎ 02 835 72 25;
🕙 9am-1am Mon-Sat, 2pm-1am Sun; per
hour €2.80) Alzaia Naviglio Pavese 2 (2,
B6; Ⓜ Garibaldi) Viale Tunisia 11 (2, E3;
Ⓜ Stazione Centrale)
Phone Point (2, B5; ☎ 02 894 20 713;
💻 www.phonepoint.com; Via Vigevano
20; per hour €3)
Rivareno (☎ 02 890 77 147; Viale Col
di Lana 8) Offers free Internet access with
gelato purchase.

USEFUL WEBSITES
The Lonely Planet website www.lonely
planet.com links to Milan's most helpful
websites.
Milan Daily (💻 www.milandaily.com)
Milan-related news in English.
Tourist Office of Milan (💻 www.milano
infotourist.com) English listings for
tourism, entertainment and business.

Metric System
The metric system is standard. To allevi-
ate confusion: Italians use commas to
mark decimals, and points to indicate
thousands.

Money
CURRENCY
Italy's currency is the Euro. Bills come in de-
nominations of €500, €200, €100, €50, €20,
€10 and €5; there are coins for €2 and €1,
plus 50, 20, 10, 5, 2 and 1 cents.

TRAVELLERS CHEQUES
If the wait's too long at the bank, try a
cambio (money changer) – but don't pay
over the 3% bank commission.

CREDIT CARDS
Visa and MasterCard are the most widely
accepted cards in Italy. Small hotels and
many restaurants sometimes don't accept
cards. For 24-hour card cancellations or
assistance, call the number on the back of
your card.

American Express ☎ 800 874 333
Diners Club ☎ 800 864 064
MasterCard ☎ 800 870 866
Visa ☎ 800 877 232

ATMS
You'll get better exchange rates withdraw-
ing Euros with your ATM card than you
would at a *cambio* (money changer). If your
bank charges fees for foreign withdrawals,
withdraw the maximum.

CHANGING MONEY
Try your ATM, a *cambio*, or these exchange
services:
American Express (3, E5; ☎ 02 721 04
010; Via Larga 4; 🕙 9am-5.30pm Mon-Fri;
Ⓜ Duomo)
Banca Cesare Ponte (3, C5; Piazza del
Duomo 19; Ⓜ Duomo)
Banca Commerciale Italiana (3, C3;
Piazza della Scala; Ⓜ Montenapoleone)

Newspapers & Magazines
You can buy all major European and US pub-
lications at bigger newsstands. Two handy
English-language papers are *Hello Milano*
(www.hellomilano.it) and *Easy Milano*
(www.easymilano.it). For the real scoop on
Milan in Italian, try:
2Night (💻 www.2night.it)
Corriere della Sera's Vivi Milano
(💻 www.corriere.it/vivimilano)
Mousse (💻 www.moussemagazine.it)
OK Arte Milano (💻 www.okarte.net)
Urban (💻 www.urbanmagazine.it)
Zero2 (💻 www.zeronline.it)

Opening Hours
Except for August holidays, most establish-
ments have regular business hours. Shops
in central Milan usually open from 3pm
to 7pm Monday and from 10am to 7pm
Tuesday to Saturday, but elsewhere most
are closed from 1pm to 3.30pm. Museums
and galleries mostly close on Mondays.
Banks open from 8.30am to 1.30pm and

3.30pm to 4.30pm weekdays. Cafés open from 7.30am until around 8pm or later, while restaurants open for lunch from noon till 3pm; dinner is usually from 7pm until midnight. Clubs open from around 10pm until 3am or 4am.

Photography & Video
Even if you ask nicely, photography is usually forbidden in Milan's boutiques, and flash photography prohibited at tourist sites. Film, memory cards and other photography accessories are available at **FNAC** (3, B6; ☎ 02 720 03 354;   cnr Via della Palla 2 & Via Torino; Ⓜ Duomo). Italy uses the PAL video system.

Post
Italy's **postal service** (💻 www.poste.it) is unreliable – entrust it with postcards, not parcels. Post offices and tobacconists sell *francobolli* (stamps).
Central Post Office (3, B4; Piazza Cordusio; ☽ 8am-7pm Mon-Fri, Sat 8.30am-noon)
Stazione Centrale (2, E2; Piazza Duca d'Aosta; ☽ 8am-7pm Mon-Fri, Sat 8.30am-12.30pm)

Radio
For music and chat, tune into state-run radio stations RAI-1 89.7 FM, RAI-2 91.7 FM or **RAI-3 93.7AM** (💻 www.radio.rai.it). You might get hooked despite yourself on goofy Italian hip-hop and maddeningly catchy ballads on 99.7 FM and 107 FM with **Radio DJ** (💻 www.deejay.it), or **Radio Capital** (💻 www.capital.it) on 91 FM and 93.1 FM.

Telephone
Local calls are charged by the minute, and additional charges apply to calls to and from mobile phones. To avoid mobile-phone and hotel surcharges, try public payphones or call centres. Only a few public phones accept coins; most accept Telecom Italia phonecards and Unica calling cards (see below), though some public phones only accept Infostrada or Albacom cards. Call centres located around train stations and in student areas charge by the minute for calls to local, international and mobile-phone numbers – mobile phone calls often cost more than international ones.

PHONE CARDS
Phone cards from **Telecom Italia** and **Unica** (☎ 800 341 341) can be used to make calls from both private and public phones. Cards can be purchased from tobacconists, newspaper stands and Telecom offices.

MOBILE PHONES
You can purchase a *prepagato* (prepaid) account for your GSM, dual- or tri-band mobile phone from TIM (Telecom Italia Mobile) or Omnitel. Package deals are also offered by Wind and Blu. All four providers sell SIM cards (giving you an Italian mobile-phone number) and *ricarica* (prepaid calling cards). To buy a SIM card, you'll need your passport and an address in Italy.

COUNTRY & CITY CODES
Milan's 02 city code must be dialled before local numbers; mobile numbers have no initial 0.

Italy	☎ 39
Milan	☎ 02

USEFUL PHONE NUMBERS

Cinemas & museums	☎ 1101
Hotels & ATMs	☎ 1102
International directory enquiries	☎ 176
International operator	☎ 170
Local operator & directory enquiries	☎ 12
Reverse-charge (collect)	☎ 170
Pharmacies	☎ 100

Television

With its seminudity, nonsensical variety shows and reality programs specialising in public humiliation, Italian television has a certain cringe-inducing, 'can they do that on TV?' appeal. State-run television stations RAI-1, RAI-2 and RAI-3 are competing with the local Milan stations and private Canale 5, Italia 1, Rete 4 and La 7 stations to provide a steady stream of salacious silliness and the odd worthwhile programme (often on RAI-3). Many hotels have satellite television, but English programming is generally limited to BBC World and CNN.

Time

Milan Standard Time is one hour ahead of GMT/UTC; daylight savings apply.

Tipping

When service isn't included on your bill, leave a 10% to 15% tip. If service is included, you can leave a tad extra for good service. In bars, you can leave small change as a tip. Tipping isn't expected by taxi drivers, but staff at swanky hotels are another story.

Toilets

Skip the sketchy public toilets and head for the nearest café or bar – a clean bathroom is worth the price of a coffee.

Tourist Information

Central Tourist Office (3, C5; ☎ 02 725 24 301; ▭ www.milanoinfotourist.com; Via Marconi 1; ☙ 8.45am-1pm & 2-6pm Mon-Sat, 9am-1pm & 2-5pm Sun; Ⓜ Duomo)
Linate Airport (4, B3; ☎ 02 702 00 443; ☙ 9am-5pm Mon-Fri)
Malpensa Airport (4, A2; ☎ 02 748 67 213; ☙ 9am-5pm Mon-Fri)
Stazione Centrale (2, E2; ☎ 02 725 24 360; ☙ 8am-7pm Mon-Sat, 9am-noon & 1.30-6pm Sun)

Women Travellers

Milan is a city of flirts, both male and female – but if the charm wears off, walk away. If you should ever feel threatened, approach a police officer or *carabinieri*.

LANGUAGE

Do not confuse local shyness about speaking English with aloofness in Milan – try a few words of Italian, and suddenly you're on friendly terms. Grab Lonely Planet's *Italian Phrasebook* and road-test some phrases.

Basics

Hello.	*Buongiorno.* (pol)
	Ciao. (inf)
Goodbye.	*Arrivederci.* (pol)
	Ciao. (inf)
Yes.	*Sì.*
No.	*No.*
Please.	*Per favore/*
	Per piacere.
Thank you.	*Grazie.*
You're welcome.	*Prego.*
Excuse me.	*Scusi.*
I'm sorry.	*Mi dispiace.*
Do you speak English?	*Parla inglese?*
I don't understand.	*Non capisco.*
How much is this?	*Quanto costa*
	questo?

Getting Around

When does ... leave/	*A che ora parte/*
arrive?	*arriva ...?*
the bus	*l'autobus*
the train	*il treno*
I'd like a ... ticket.	*Vorrei un biglietto*
	di ...
one way	*solo andata*
return	*andata e ritorno*
Where is ...?	*Dov'è è ...?*
Go straight ahead.	*Si va sempre diritto.*
Turn left/right.	*Giri a sinistra/destra.*

Accommodation
a hotel	un albergo
Do you have any rooms available?	Avete delle camere libere?
with a bathroom	con (un) bagno

Do you have a … room?	Avete una camera …
single	singola
twin	doppia
double	matrimoniale

Eating
breakfast	prima colazione
lunch	pranzo
dinner	cena
The bill, please	Il conto, per favore

Entertainment
What's on …?	Che c'è in programma …?
locally	in zona
this weekend	questo fine settimana
today	oggi
tonight	stasera

Shopping
| I'm just looking. | Sto solo guardando. |

Do you accept …?	Accettate …?
credit cards	carte di credito
travellers cheques	assegni per viaggiatori

Internet
| Where's the local internet café? | Dove si trova l'internet point? |

I'd like to …	Vorrei …
check my email	controllare le mie email
get online	collegarmi a internet

Around Town
I'm looking for …	Sto cercando …
the market	il mercato
a public toilet	un gabinetto pubblico
the tourist office	l'ufficio di turismo

| What time does it open/close? | A che ora si apre/chiude? |

Where's the nearest …?	Dov'è il … più vicino?
ATM	bancomat
foreign exchange office	cambio

Time, Days & Numbers
What time is it?	Che ora è?
today	oggi
tomorrow	domani
yesterday	ieri
morning	mattina
afternoon	pomeriggio
day	giorno

Monday	lunedì
Tuesday	martedì
Wednesday	mercoledì
Thursday	giovedì
Friday	venerdì
Saturday	sabato
Sunday	domenica

1	uno
2	due
3	tre
4	quattro
5	cinque
6	sei
7	sette
8	otto
9	nove
10	dieci
100	cento
1000	mille

Index

See also separate subindexes for Eating (p93), Entertainment (p93), Shopping (p93), Sights with map references (p94) and Sleeping (p94).